GAA
Confidential

Everything you never
knew you wanted to know
about Gaelic games

Darragh McManus is from Tipperary. He writes for the *Irish Independent* and *Evening Herald*, and previously edited *High Ball* GAA magazine. He loves films, literature, conversation, music, philosophy, sport, daydreaming and smoking cigarettes. His ambition is to graciously refuse an Oscar for Best Director. He agrees that beauty is truth and vice versa.

GAA
Confidential

Everything you never knew you wanted to know about Gaelic games

DARRAGH McMANUS

HODDER
HEADLINE
IRELAND

Copyright © 2007, Darragh McManus

First published in 2007 by Hodder Headline Ireland

1

The right of Darragh McManus to be identified as the Author of the Work
has been asserted by him in accordance with the Copyright, Designs
and Patents Act, 1988.

A CIP catalogue record for this title is available from the British Library.

ISBN 978 0340 93808 9

Typeset by Anú Design, Tara
Cover and text design by Anú Design, Tara
Printed and bound in Great Britain by Clays Ltd, St Ives plc

Hodder Headline Ireland's policy is to use papers that are natural,
renewable and recyclable products and made from wood grown in
sustainable forests. The logging and manufacturing processes are expected
to conform to the environmental regulations of the country of origin.

Earlier versions of some of these pieces were previously published
in *High Ball* magazine. Despite best efforts, the author and publisher
have been unable to contact all copyright holders. We would encourage
copyright holders of material not acknowledged to contact us.

Hodder Headline Ireland
8 Castlecourt Centre
Castleknock
Dublin 15
Ireland

www.hhireland.ie

www.gaaconfidential.com

A division of Hachette Livre, 338 Euston Road, London NW1 3BH, England

Contents

The games

The competitions

The fans

The media

The arts and culture

The look

The other stuff that wouldn't fit anywhere else

The boardgame

The introduction

WELCOME
to MY WORLD

The Gaelic Athletic Association is one of the most successful and vibrant amateur sports bodies in the world, and has been a seminal influence on Irish life since its inception in 1884. In the face of official and casual hostility, poverty and mass emigration, infinite counter-attractions and a post-colonial inferiority complex the size of Mongolia, it has thrived, evolved and endured. It is, in many ways, the soul of Ireland.

Now cut the uileann pipes, fellas; that's enough myth-making. The greatest thing about the GAA isn't its rich history or the way it continues to keep alive our indigenous culture in the face of a McGlobal onslaught. No – the GAA is great because it's a living, breathing, vital part of the everyday life of hundreds of thousands of people on this island and abroad. On an individual, community and national basis, we determine ourselves primarily through our connection to this enormous latticework of like-minded souls. I mean, if I had to choose between Ireland winning the soccer World Cup and my county winning even a provincial title, I'd choose the latter any time.

Someone once told me that, should he be interviewing two job candidates of equal capability and experience, he would almost certainly give the position to whichever of them was a 'good GAA man'. (If they're both good GAA men, you throw a contract in the air and let them fight for possession by the filing desk.) And I can totally dig that. Growing up, I metered my year around playing matches, going to matches, waiting for the next season. The inter-county championship completely defined the summer for me, and still does to a large extent. My lifelong ambition, once I realised I'd never actually captain a team to an All-Ireland, was to sponsor the county jersey with the logo of my wildly successful movie production company. Which, you know, I'm still hopeful of if that bastard Scorsese ever returns my email.

The GAA is more than a sporting organisation. It's cultural, it's social, it's political, it's spiritual; hell, it's metaphysical if you're inclined to think that way. And best of all, it's the most hugely welcoming body of people I've ever encountered, which would explain how an ungrateful little punk like me can affectionately poke fun at it for the next few hundred pages and get away with it.

This is my homage to everything that makes the GAA special: the games, the people, the excitement and fun, the triumphs and disasters, the momentous and the ridiculous.

Cumann Lúthchleas Gael abú!

About the author

The author's principal memory of his first GAA match, an U9 football tournament (author aged seven), was getting smashed in the nose with the ball. Insult was added to injury when he was taken off soon after … shamefully, by his *own father*. He went on to enjoy an underage career of mixed fortunes, including the longest losing run in his club's history, the longest non-scoring run in his club's history, and quite possibly the ten largest margins of defeat in his club's history. His finest/worst hour came when, in a fit of pique at the management, he refused to attend a divisional minor final, choosing instead to visit a neighbouring village in the hope of meeting cute babes.

All this was bookended with a few divisional titles, a lot of fun and, here and there, the odd excellent performance and memorable moment – a perfect overhead connection, the thrill of a well-taken goal – which made the whole thing worthwhile. His career fizzled out, strangely, around the time he discovered the joys of smoking, girls, daytime television marathons and monumental laziness … aah, college life. The author's last match was a minor hurling fixture, during which his chronic lack of fitness and sorely reduced lung capacity proved equally insurmountable handicaps. Unsurprisingly, the team lost again.

He has since carved out an unremarkable career in journalism, which included a stint editing a national GAA magazine and writing on nearly every subject known to man (such as unrealistic movie character names, celebrity haircuts, parliamentary violence in Venezuela and the favourite subject of any self-respecting hack: himself). He has written some fiction (unpublished), movie scripts (unfilmed) and overwrought poetry (unread and unlamented). The author has also published work under a range of pseudonyms, including Alex O'Hara, Dutch Mastourakis, Mike Skinner the King of Kelmorg and, in the case of threatening letters to various public figures, a large 'X' scrawled in his own blood.

He is currently working on a Dadaist comedy based on the lives of several notorious county board officials. He remains a member of his home club.

Reasons for writing this book

1. The GAA has been ill served by the written word through the ages. Where soccer had Albert Camus, boxing had Norman Mailer and rugby had Tony Ward's autobiography, the greatest games of them all, with a few notable exceptions, have been ignored by the literati.

2. This seems a particular shame, considering Ireland's well-earned reputation for literary excellence. Historically, our playwrights have given a tough but fair shoulder to the English, our novelists have pulled hard on the French and our poets have slyly tugged the jersey of the Italians, then swooned to the ground in a cloud of melancholic pique. But seeing as how Yeats, Shaw and Jemmy

Joyce each seems to have forgotten to craft their GAA-based *meisterwerk*, I guess it's up to me.

3. Sport, and its attendant cultural and social expression, is simultaneously far too important and far too ludicrous to be left in the hands of unimaginative writers who can't move beyond a prosaic recording of the facts or, worse, seek a laughable 'meaning' in every belt of a ball. I aim to honour the absurdity, beauty and sheer fun of it all.

4. There is no such person as the average GAA fan. Contrary to popular assumption, it has always been a breathtakingly broad church, straddling social strata, occupational and educational differences and, to a lesser extent, the rural/urban divide. For every stereotypical farmer swinging a hurley, there was a doctor or dolehead booting the leather.

5. This is also a (very) belated riposte to the girl who told me, during my college heyday of floppy hair, Paisley shirts, feminist ideology, gay rights and avant-garde musical tastes, 'You don't seem like someone who'd be into GAA.' Sorry – why not, exactly?

6. The association has changed over time. And the young(ish), professional, well-travelled, philosophising, drug-dabbling, gig-going, pop-culture-addled GAA person – someone whose world view was formed as much by cartoons, technology, foreign films and third-level education as by their locality and history – deserves to have his or her experience, and equal love for our culture, recorded too.

7. This book might also have the happy benefit of educating certain culturally enslaved morons in Irish society about the reality of the GAA: that we're not *all* God-fearing, anti-contraception, Semtex-toting woollybacks with crossed eyes and an inability to do simple subtraction. (Just some of us.)

8. Nobody ever writes on all the associated crap and nonsense that many of us think about: the imaginary movies that were never made, the heroically awful haircuts of certain decades, how *Sunday Game* clichés translate into Portuguese, etc., etc. So I'm going to.

9. To smash the misconceptions, damn the ignorant, glorify the glorious and bestow a cheerful 'fuck you' on the begrudgers.
10. For the money. Obviously.

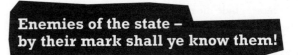

Enemies of the state – by their mark shall ye know them!

The following unsavoury sorts will assuredly, come the revolution and the creation of my benevolent dictatorship in Ireland, be first up against the proverbial wall.

- Anyone who uses the words 'dinosaurs', 'backwoodsmen' or 'bigots' when discussing the GAA.

- Anyone who constantly lambasts administrators who have devoted countless hours of voluntary service.

- Anyone who thinks the GAA is sectarian against Protestants.

- Anyone who automatically assumes all GAA people are religious hardliners and social *über*-conservatives.

- Anyone who insists on calling football 'Gaelic' and soccer 'football'.

- Anyone who calls hurling 'stickfighting' and football 'bogball'.

- Anyone who mispronounces 'hurling' as 'hurdling'.

- Anyone who refers to a hurley as a 'hurley stick'.

- Anyone who prizes the global entertainment industry that is professional sport (particularly soccer) over their indigenous culture.

- Anyone who is ashamed of that culture to the extent they would sooner see it die than embrace it.

- Anyone who thinks they're better than GAA people because they follow a foreign sports franchise instead of their local hurling and football club.

- Anyone who thinks they're sophisticated because they know the names of Arsenal's manager or the French prop-forward, but not the names of the last two All-Ireland winning captains.

- Anyone who pretends not to know anything about GAA in a desperate attempt to hide the fact that they grew up on a sheep-covered mountainside somewhere.

- Anyone who takes pride in the fact that they've never attended a GAA match.

- Any member of the globetrotting 'Green Army' which pops up with such irritating predictability whenever Ireland qualifies for the World Cup.

- Anyone who puts international soccer or rugby success over their own county doing well.

- Anyone who knows the words to 'Ireland's Call'.

- Anyone who doesn't know the words to 'Amhrán na bhFiann'.

- Anyone who gives press prominence to the Premiership over a big Gaelic games fixture.

- Anyone who sees the GAA as the IRA at play.

- Anyone dissing the Irish language, whether they speak it or not.

- Anyone still bitter about how the Ban hobbled their (exceedingly limited) chances of a professional sports career.

- Anyone who thinks all GAA folks have thick mucker accents.

- Anyone who stupidly refers to camogie players and women's footballers as 'heifers' or unattractive, yet somehow are blinded by the beauty of hockey players with the exact same body shape.

- Anyone who constantly butts their nose into GAA affairs, making wild accusations on something they know nothing about and, by their own admission, have no interest in.

- Anyone proselytising for professionalism.

- Anyone who appears to be supportive of the GAA but in actuality is just the poison on the inside.

- Anyone who doesn't have a problem with the butcher's apron flying over Croke Park.

- Anyone who doesn't feel a swell of pride when the national anthem strikes up just before the start of a GAA match.

- Anyone who doesn't feel a swell of pride when their daughter or son's school team wins some Z-division competition or other.

- Anyone who secretly wishes Ireland had never left the United Kingdom.

- Anyone who believes that incidents like the Bloody Sunday massacre of 1920 have no relevance to the present day.

- Anyone who doesn't understand that Gaelic games are culturally more important in Ireland than other sports.

Wow. That's quite a lot of killin' to be done, ain't it?

The history

The Origin of the Species

Who would have thought, as the GAA enjoys its third century, second millennium and thirteenth decade (I think), that we'd ever get this far, given such modest origins? It wasn't all packed stadiums and TV coverage back in the old days. It wasn't even half-packed stands and limited Nickelodeon coverage. It was, rather, mostly windswept fields and one of those old box cameras with the big handheld flash, if you were lucky.

The GAA was formally founded in 1884, but its history goes back way, *waaayy* before that. Hurling, the association's crown jewel, was first mentioned in the mythology of the battle of Magh Tuireadh, near 'King' Cong in County Mayo, said to have taken place in 1272 BC. The Tuatha de Danann demanded half of Ireland from the Firbolgs – whoever

the hell any of these people were – and while the two sides were waiting to fight it out, they played a hurling match. If only all the world's conflicts and differences of opinion could be resolved so sportingly.

And the Tailteann Games took place at an even further remove. Though not originally involving hurling or football, they were the spiritual forerunners of the GAA in many ways. Like in an ignoring-work-and-any-outside-interests-to-spend-all-our-time-on-sport way, for one. Ancient Irish annals date the Games back to the death of Queen Tailte in 2500 BC, making them several centuries older than the Olympics. How d'ya like *that*, Ancient Greece!? Indeed, some writers have conjectured that the Greeks got the idea of the Olympics from the Tailteann Games, the plagiarising blighters.

Where the crass commercialisation and rampant steroid use came from is anyone's guess.

Athletics, boxing, wrestling, chariot-racing, spear-throwing and swimming all took place in the Games, as did bloody slaughtering, being irrationally frightened of thunderstorms and month-long, mead-drinking binges. Aenach Tailteann (to give it its full copyrighted name) was 'disturbed' by rival kings in AD 717 and 774 (I wonder if this involved said rival kings running around in scary masks and going 'Boo!'), boycotted in 811 and last staged by Ruaidrí Ua Conchobair in 1167. But it's heartening to note that the peasantry kept up the habit of drinking and fighting in honour of the Games right up until, well, yesterday.

I Need a Hero

Presenting the ultimate GAA superheroes from the past

Name: Cuchulainn

Club: Red Hand Gaels

Position: Demi-god

Honours: Permanent place in legend; subject of odes and sagas recounted by men with wild facial hair; Junior B football league

Born: Misty mists of time

Great life and mighty deeds: Made mark early on, winning Accurate Puck Competition by belting a sliotar into a hound's jaws. Prize included Nissubishi Chariot 1.8L and year's supply of moisturising magic potions. Changed name by deed poll from Setanta to Cuchulainn. Defeated Connacht champion Ferdia in injury-time in Mighty Warrior Slugfest. Stormy relationship for several years with Queen Maeve, well-known society belle. Nadir reached when implicated in infamous payment-of-stolen-bull-for-play scandal. Transferred to small intermediate club in The Waters and the Wild. Came out of retirement at advanced age (702) for one last stab, saying, 'We want this wan badly, we have the hunger, and we're going to do it if it kills me.' Unfortunately, it killed him.

◊◊◊

Name: Fionn MacCumhaill (also known by stage name of Finn McCool)

Club: Na Fianna (no connection to the Glasnevin outfit)

Position: Roaming all over the country (often in one afternoon)

Honours: Mention in Flann O'Brien novel; primary schools' runner-up medal; straddled game like colossus – literally

Born: Fadó, fadó

Great life and mighty deeds: Orphaned after parents eaten by giant wolf and reared in Knights of Fianna Home for Young Heroes. Prowess with camán nurtured by Christian Brother from Offaly. Finest stickman of his generation, using arse the size of a ➡

house to shield possession, while his ability to run under stick three inches off the ground enabled him to break clear of the pack. Intoned twelve books of ancient poetry to win Scór recitation prize. During International Rules series with some troll or something from England, Fionn made the space, took one look at the posts and hurled part of Antrim at his opponent, squashing him and creating the Isle of Man in the process. Intra-club factions later developed when fiancée, Gráinne, fell in love with team-mate, Diarmuid. Enraged Fionn eventually relented, after burning thumb on lunch (lovely piece of magic fish) and receiving much wisdom.

Name: Wolfe Tone

Club: Wolfe Tones (obviously)

Position: Revolutionary high ground

Honours: Iconic status; subject of republican come-all-ye's; gave name to many pubs

Born: Not so fadó

Great life and mighty deeds: Thinking man's player, well-versed in political ideology. Dressing-room speeches particularly inspiring for team-mates (or 'brothers in the common struggle', as he insisted on calling them). Much emphasis on teamwork, hence inclusion of Protestants and Catholics in team selections. Quoted as saying, 'I mean, like, we have a small pick here in Ireland, so you can't be choosy. It's well and good for the likes of the British Empire to pick and choose; the so-called "weaker countries" have to make do.' Caused minor stir as first prominent player to wear ponytail and velvet pantaloons on pitch. Career unfortunately cut short by execution by fierce rivals, Britain Óg, under contentious new 'Insurrection' rule. Harsh treatment surprisingly not denounced at following year's congress.

5

Hurling through time

Hurling, of course, has a heritage richer than the lovechild of Steven Spielberg and that cat who owns Wal-Mart. Most of the ancient mythological heroes are said to have played *iománíocht*, like Cuchulainn and Fionn MacCumhaill, while Diarmuid actually won the heart of fair Gráinne by scoring three times in a match, which makes her the first GAA trophy wife, I suppose.

The Brehon Laws – the legal code of Ireland until the fifteenth century when those imperialist tramps arsed it all up for us – codified hurling and provided for compensation in case of accident. Amusingly, specific rules were set down on such issues as how, exactly, players should retrieve the ball from a field (seek permission to enter the land, close the gate when leaving and avoid the shotgun-waving irate farmer), and the proper metal from which one's hurley hoop should be made (bronze for a king's son, copper for the plebs). Under the Brehon Laws, a hurley couldn't even be confiscated, but then the Normans had to swan in with their killjoy edicts. Literally – it was, 'Have any joy and we'll kill you.' The 1367 Statute of Kilkenny banned hurling on the grounds that settlers should instead be preparing for war by practising their archery. They'd obviously never seen the typical Junior C corner-back in full blood-crazed mode.

In the middle of the last millennium, some landlords had 'stables' of hurlers (who, appropriately, were forced to sleep in straw and subsist on horse poo), and huge wagers were laid on inter-county and inter-provincial matches by dipsomaniac heirs determined to squander the family estate before its liquid consumption murdered their liver. One 1769 encounter carried the not inconsiderable prize of 300 guineas, though the poor old hurlers, after belting a ball and each other from parish to parish for several hours, generally had to make do with a few barrels of ale. And to think how the top players moan nowadays about making sacrifices.

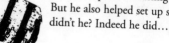

This noble pursuit even got a mention in Brian Merriman's epic poem *Cuirt an Mhean Oiche*, but the Great Famine (1845–47) killed much of the interest in hurling (along with much of the population of Ireland). Thus, the game declined among the common folk, until its revival in the late nineteenth century: first through the establishment of the Trinity College Hurley Union and then Michael Cusack's foundation of the Metropolitan Hurling Club in Dublin. But he also helped set up something else, didn't he? Indeed he did…

Foundation once again

Dateline: 1 November 1884. Opium dens fill with effete playwrights and bored aristocrats. A spooky fog rolls in from the Thames and covers London. Émile Zola debates whether on not to pack in this whole writing lark and take up that offer of a job with his uncle's painting and decorating firm. And, in the billiards room of Hayes Hotel in Thurles, seven people convene to establish the Gaelic Athletic Association.

Among them, of course, were cultural revivalist and Karl Marx lookalike, Michael Cusack, first president Maurice Davin, and all-round Renaissance man John Wyse-Power, who was an IRB member, editor of the *Leinster Leader* and athletics devotee. He may or may not also have found time to present a cookery and gardening programme on local radio. Most of the first meeting, oddly enough, was taken up discussing athletics. Cusack had an idea for a national athletics body, governed by the people, for the people and of the people (those mightn't have been his exact words). He also proposed a Celtic athletics festival to raise funds for the fledgling body. The meeting, as they say, was adjourned.

It wasn't until the following year that rules were drawn up for football and hurling, but it's been onwards and upwards ever since. Clara quickly became the first club to join the Metropolitan Hurling Club in the new association. In January 1885, Killimor defeated Ballinakill in the first hurling match. In February, three football matches were played. And, in November, the first convention was held, with representatives from 300 clubs. Cusack was reported to have described the early growth of the association as being 'like a prairie fire'. Which is apt, really, because the dude also resembled macho frontiersman poet Walt Whitman.

The first inter-county match took place between Galway and North Tipperary in February 1886. The hurlers arrived at the Phoenix Park where – in a fore-shadowing of the prejudice and bullshit we'd have to put up with for the next century – the stupid gatekeeper had locked the gates, forewarned that 'a mob with battering rams' was bent on mayhem and destruction. Thankfully, a Victorian version of Ger Loughnane wasn't required to wrench the gates from the ground and contemptuously toss them aside; the gatekeeper was just given a sedative and the players proceeded inside.

County boards were introduced in 1886 and, the following year, ➤

the All-Ireland championships were first organised, each county represented by their champion clubs. Only five counties competed in hurling and eight in football. Lazy feckers. What else did they have to do that was so pressing? The first hurling championship match was between Meelick and Castlebridge of Wexford, while the first football championship match saw Dundalk Young Irelands play Ballyduff Lower from Waterford. That's right, I said Louth and Waterford. Interestingly – and not a little disturbingly – if a player fouled another in those early days, the two would wrestle on the field of play. I'm not making this up: they would actually wrestle each other. Presumably, they would then repair to the dressing room for some sexual braggadocio and heavy-duty nipple-tweaking. (See also under H for Homoerotic Tendencies.)

In 1888, the first All-Ireland hurling final was played in Birr. Meelick travelled to the game by charabanc (a type of motor coach mainly used for sightseeing tours, m'lud) and togged out, only to hear that Tipperary champs Thurles were not travelling. The Galway representatives had just started into a meal when Tipp arrived, but presumably were afforded a half-hour to let their food digest before getting stuck in. At that time, a goal outweighed any number of points and if the sides were level on goals and points, the game would be decided on forfeit points, awarded in the same circumstances as a 65 today. Tipperary remembered the advice of their childhood mentors, taking their forfeit points while letting the goals take care of themselves. Or goal, anyway. They finished with one of each, thus winning the first title on the unique scoreline of 1–1–1 to 0.

Their likes won't be seen again … especially not the charabanc.

Michael Cusack: a life less ordinary

1847:
Born in Carron, County Clare.

1870:
Tentative first steps in growing a beard

1874:
Facial hair reaches full, magnificent bushiness.

1866:
Becomes first principal of Lough Cutra National School in Galway.

1871:
Teaches maths, commerce and English at St Colman's in Newry.

1876:
Marries Margaret Woods from County Down.

1882:
Begins writing column in *The Shamrock*, possibly on beard maintenance.

Still 1881:
Proposes new body to control Irish athletics.

Also 1882:
Forms Gaelic Union for the Preservation and Cultivation of the Irish language, resulting in publication of *Gaelic Journal*.

Also 1881:
Becomes passionately interested in athletics. Boy, he was fickle.

1881:
Just as oddly, now preaches doctrine of cricket, even advocating it as Irish game. This infatuation later leads to GAA tradition of white coats for umpires.

1883:
Founds Dublin Hurling Club. Unfortunately, it lasts just four months.

1884:
Culmination of self-styled 'Gaelic mission' – proposal for establishment of GAA.

1879:
Establishes the Civil Service Academy Hurley Club and, oddly, a rugby team.

1891:
Facial shrubbery begins to show a bit of grey.

1906:
At his death, is described as 'living embodiment of GAA'.

1878:
Founds a school in Dublin to assist young people entering civil service or universities. Cusack teaches all subjects and even publishes his own question-and-answer books, the brainiac.

1922:
James Joyce's epic triumph of literary bravado and gobbledegook, *Ulysses*, published in Paris. The character of The Citizen, an anti-Semitic dickhead, is reckoned to have been based on Cusack. But what did Joyce know, the specky git?

1984:
Birthplace restored by GAA. Last resting place of dismembered beard remains closely guarded secret.

Also 1876:
Trims back beard slightly in spirit of marital compromise. .

Vive la République!

As long ago as 1641, Gaelic games were being linked to what was seen by the crown as seditious activity. That year, the President of Munster — really, that was his title — claimed that 'papists' were assembling in Tipperary 'under pretence of a hurling match'. The Lord Lieutenant wailed in 1798 that football matches were used to disguise meetings of the United Irishmen. Even Daniel O'Connell, the Emancipation-*meister* himself, declared in 1831 that political meetings were being held, disguised as 'hurling or other amusements'.

The insinuation that the GAA is basically a training ground for armed terrorists persists to this day, with our more excitable commentators stopping just short of announcing that Gerry Adams is the puppet-master controlling it all and that Croke Park houses a weapons stash beneath the new conference centre. The reality, of course, is and was far less dramatic, and many of the assumed certainties are simply incorrect. Cusack, for instance, has been decried as anti-Semitic and anti-Protestant; he was neither and didn't support IRB violence. And the GAA wasn't set up as cover for republican activity — its aim was to prevent indigenous pastimes and arts from slipping into extinction. I mean, it's a ridiculous contention that this elaborate cover would be established for revolutionary endeavours. With all that effort put into establishing the GAA, they wouldn't have had any energy left over for fighting.

Anyway, yes, some of the early figures of prominence were involved with the Fenians or IRB, but so what? Ireland was under the colonial thumb of Britain, wasn't it? It had been degraded to the status of sweatshop of the Empire. All peoples have the right to self-determination. (Or does that only apply to non-Irish insurgents?) And the British had to be forcibly turfed out of every country they ever occupied. Frankly, I don't see the problem here. These men and women were doing nothing more or less than any of their enlightened peers — taking arms against an oppressor who wouldn't listen to reasonable argument. And it makes sense that the same people who were politically nationalist should also be culturally nationalist, just as the lackeys grazing on the master's table droppings couldn't have given a damn about their native culture.

If anything, they should be commended for their actions, sparing us a century of royal rule, decline, upheaval, Thatcherite government and Rupert Murdoch. Thanks, folks.

Citius, altius, fortius

The GAA was one of the earliest national athletics body to be established, which would explain the full name of the association but doesn't quite elucidate why there are absolutely no athletics involved today. Personally, I put it down to the fact that running, jumping and throwing things were exceedingly popular in Victorian times – they had to discharge all that pent-up sexual energy somehow – but diminished in popularity as we moved into the twentieth century. The founders probably believed that athletics would continue to exert a magnetic hold on the collective imagination, when in reality everyone gradually realised they could have much more fun chasing a ball around a field.

Regardless, these sweatsome pursuits played an important role in establishing the GAA during the early years, with athletics meetings helping promote the nascent organisation. In October 1885, an All-Ireland athletics championship was staged, and at least two world records were set at GAA meetings during the first twelve months. In fact, I don't know what in blazes they were putting in the tea, but Irish athletes were world-beaters back then, in poignant contrast to our current crop who couldn't win an Olympic medal if the rest of the field had their running shoes tied together.

Maurice Davin, for instance, held the world hammer record when the association was founded, but he wasn't the only one. Over half the world track-and-field records were held by Irishmen at the turn of the twentieth century. Davin's brother Pat actually came out of retirement to hold six different world records at one stage, while several robust fellows swapped the long-jump record between them for a few years. Remarkably, not to mention hilariously, Peter O'Connor's record stood as the Irish benchmark until 1990. GAA men also have a proud history of excellence in the Olympic Games, bestriding the event like veritable sporting gods. Unfortunately, they were representing another country at the time (this being because Ireland didn't properly exist). Four GAA athletes won gold at the London Olympics in 1908, and two more followed up in Stockholm four years later. Sadly, though these men were Irish in heart and mind, none of the victories are credited to Ireland. Sob.

Down all the days

From great saplings do mighty acorns spring. Or something like that. And the GAA, after a shaky enough start – the founders didn't quite seem to know where they were headed with all of this – has gone from strength to strength, growing into the ass-kickin', mother-lovin', heart-breakin' and life-takin' sporting Goliath we all know and love today.

Many twists have been taken along the road; many turns of fortune's wheel, climbs and falls, dips and precipices. Now, for me to detail what, exactly, occurred during that first century or so would take far more effort than I'm prepared to devote to you lot. It'd also make this into a history book, as opposed to whatever kind of book it currently is. I feel it's better, therefore, to skip through the particulars and just give a general overview of each decade since, I dunno, let's say the 1900s, framed within a wider subtext. And better yet, to do so in the style of popular TV nostalgia orgy, *Reeling in the Years*, wherein some catchy music forms the backdrop to a brisk skim through all the major happenings. Hit it.

Memorable moments in world history

12 billion BC: Universe created from nothing in infinitely huge explosion. Arrangements for first championship still at committee stage.

6 billion BC: First hurling final played between self-replicating single cell amoeba and itself. Ends in draw. (Unsurprisingly.)

1900s

What happened in music: The use of Hawaiian-style slide guitar became popular in country music.

What happened in world affairs: Henry Ford revolutionised industrial production with the Model T.

What happened in GAA: All-Ireland finals were still being played several years out of synch. Groan.

1910s

What happened in music: 'Oh Susanna' lorded it over all others at the top of the charts.

What happened in world affairs: Youth and hope drowned in the killing fields of the Somme.

What happened in GAA: The GAA bought a site in Jones Road, Dublin, from one Frank Dineen and named it Croke Park.

600 million BC:
Tyrannosaurus Gaels face off against Velociraptor Dan Breens, using prehistoric conifers as hurleys and dead armadillo as ball. Jeff Goldblum referees.

2 million BC:
Cro-magnon man belts opposite number on head with club. Confusion reigns as to whether or not this means he wants to marry injured party.

1920s

What happened in music: Jazz began spreading from black, inner-city clubs to a wider audience.

What happened in world affairs: Some pompous old buffoon stumbled upon the tomb of King Tutankhamun, bringing a terrible curse upon his head.

What happened in GAA: The Tailteann Games were revived but didn't last very long.

1930s

What happened in music: Militarist marching bands enjoyed an upsurge in popularity throughout much of Europe.

What happened in world affairs: Hitler invaded Poland, Czechoslovakia and a bunch of other countries, the pup.

What happened in GAA: The great Mick Mackey led Limerick to two hurling All-Irelands and an unprecedented five leagues in a row (people still cared about the league back then).

Some-time-in-the-past-that's-a-bit-hard-to-work-out-exact-date BC:
Whole season rained off owing to torrential flood sent by God to punish mankind.

1500 BC: Allegations of intimidation after King Ramses II decrees that any slave who dares tackle one of royal cats will be entombed alive. Predictably enough, cats win comfortably.

1940s

What happened in music: Zoot suits became the couture of choice for swing bands.

What happened in world affairs: America detonated the first A-bomb at the alkali flats of Alamogordo.

What happened in GAA: Too much Brylcreem played havoc with players' control of the ball during wet weather and actually decided the result of at least three championships.

1950s

What happened in music: Elvis cut his first record at Sun Studios.

What happened in world affairs: Everybody, male or female, wore their hair with approximately half a pint of starch in it.

What happened in GAA: The record crowd for an All-Ireland hurling final was set by Cork and Wexford (please check in your own time whether this has subsequently been broken).

29 AD: Video evidence needed to decide whether late effort from Pádraig Herod crossed line before ball was miraculously turned into jug of wine by net-minder Jesus.

600–1200: No matches during Dark Ages because everyone really repressed and sport seen as sinful and work of devil.

1960s

What happened in music: Everybody started dropping acid and creating bizarre, inter-dimensional soundscapes, man.

What happened in world affairs: Everybody started dropping acid and creating bizarre, inter-dimensional soundscapes, man.

What happened in GAA: Down became the first team from the occupied Six Counties to win a senior All-Ireland.

1970s

What happened in music: ELO released the longest album in human history, requiring fifteen months to listen to in its entirety.

What happened in world affairs: Flares straddled the globe like a giant, omnipresent deity made out of tartan-patterned acrylic.

What happened in GAA: The legendary Kerry team tussled with the legendary Dublin team in several legendary encounters. Really, they were.

1580: John Proctor scores suspiciously wondrous point. Found guilty of transgressing association's Occult and Satanic Practices Code; receives hefty fine and burning at stake.

1789: Head of foppish French aristocrat, Baron Louis-Pierre de Montebanque, falls off late in game. He comments, 'I'd been guillotined by revolutionaries at training on Thursday night, but hoped to run it off.'

1980s

What happened in music: Synthesisers and asymmetrical fringes dominated popular culture.

What happened in world affairs: The threat of thermonuclear annihilation dissipated somewhat with the fall of communism.

What happened in GAA: With his goal against Kerry, Seamus Darby became the most famous Offaly man since ... actually, there are no other famous Offaly people.

1990s

What happened in music: The divine Kurt did live and die and was reborn.

What happened in world affairs: The US military finally allowed the rest of the world to experience that worldwide information highway super-web thing.

What happened in GAA: Hurling experienced a revolution of sorts mid-decade. Things have gone back to normal since then, though.

1932: Pablo Picasso commissioned to take official team pictures. Some consider avant-garde portraits a flattering improvement on reality.

1966: Counter-culture conspiranoiacs denounce All-Ireland final as 'tool of oppression'. Also claim one of Tony Doran's goals in recent game was a fake reconstructed in Arizona film studio.

2000s

What happened in music: The plague of the boyband finally began to recede.

What happened in world affairs: Bush announced his so-called 'war on terror', but *still* hasn't addressed my crippling fear of an (admittedly unlikely) attack of giant scorpions.

What happened in GAA: The football qualifier system was declared a resounding success, while the jury remained out on the hurling one.

2010s (hopefully)

What happened in music: The triumphant return of skiffle.

What happened in world affairs: Universal peace and understanding and, like, fellowship and love and that.

What happened in GAA: Rule 42 brought back in.

1983: Future of association thrown into doubt when entire world becomes obsessed with yo-yos and Rubik's cube. Televised appeal from Kojak brings everyone to their senses.

2130: Cytron ZX4, self-aware computo-humanoid, gives match-winning performance on Jupiter. Cause helped when human opposition all die from literal lack of atmosphere.

18

The set-up

This is how we do things around here

Someone once described the GAA as the world's greatest democracy, though I don't think he meant it in the sense that we are now a bona fide threat to Uncle Sam's global domination. He meant that, literally, every one of hundreds of thousands of members has a voice in deciding what direction the association moves in. (Although this doesn't explain how nobody paid any heed to my wild-eyed tirades about Rule 42.)

Despite some people's wilfully stupid preconceptions, the GAA is not ruled with an iron, Stalin-like fist by a tiny cabal of *apparatchiks*. It always amuses me when commentators bang on about how the GAA did this or that, to the detriment of the ordinary player, supporter or member, as if this mythical 'GAA' was a distinct body of people. The GAA *is* the people, and the people determine its future.

Every major change is decided by every member. They are ratified at the annual congress by delegates who have been mandated at county board meetings. Each club, in turn, has mandated their own delegate to those meetings. So the ordinary club member has a say even in such huge paradigm shifts as the late, lamented Rule 42 or the decade-long redevelopment of Croke Park. What other body, sporting or non, grants such real power to regular schmucks? Oh, and next time you feel the need to whinge about the 'suits' running your beloved GAA into the ground with no respect for democracy, remember: this is not a communist country. Nothing is stopping you from standing for election and getting a nice suit of your own. If you feel you've something to offer as an administrator, step up to the plate. Either way, quit *whining*.

The GAA is formally headed by the president, elected every three years, though I guess the ultimate power resides with congress. The Prez can't overrule a change to, say, the pick-up rule just because he feels like it. Although it would be funny, just once, to see a *coup* ➡

d'état take place in whatever hotel the annual gathering was located: El Presidenté marching along in his general's uniform, protestors corralled into the residents' bar and a maniacal propaganda mouthpiece babbling over the PA about 'a glorious new dawn for our people.'

Cool. Analyse *that*, Tomás.

'Obviously, Michael, they knew what they had to do and they done it today. They'll have looked at the video of the Pinochet *coup* and seen there was a lot of work to be done. But for me, the best thing was seeing all the boys and girls out in their colours, supporting the *junta*. The yellow of the tear gas, the khaki of the death-squads … it was tremenjous.'

'Thanks, Tomás. Cyril?'

'Well, these lads have been one of the top reactionary groups in the country for a long time as such, and never got the credit they deserve. Like, people will always go on about your Francos and your Baby Doc Duvaliers, but for me, these lads are as good as any of them, fellas like Paudge Peron and 'Il Fascismo' Murphy never got the credit as such…'

[Cut to ad break]

Other governing bodies include Central Council, the Games Administration Committee, provincial councils and enough work groups and sub-committees to constructively employ half of China, all overseen by the big cheese his'self, the director general. Liam Mulvihill has been DG for almost three decades now, and earned a reputation as one of the most intelligent, progressive and imaginative administrators of any grouping in this country. During his tenure, for instance, the games' popularity has soared, several contentious issues have been resolved, Croker and other grounds have been beautifully upgraded and, most importantly, the pairing of woollen bellbottoms with sparkly polo necks has been gently eased into the lay-by of history.

But forget all that. The essential point about GAA structures is that it all comes down to the club. That's the mantra everyone must memorise from a callow age: 'The club is the cornerstone of the association.' Like with the pyramids, a functioning post-autocratic society or any good kick-ass rock song, you gotta build from the bottom up.

Gimme an A, gimme a G, gimme an M

If each club is a tiny independent fiefdom within the broader organisation, the AGM is when the state of the nation is examined. This generally takes place in January, which is a handy distraction from the morbid realisation of just how depressing that month is.

At the typical AGM, power battles are waged, grievances aired, amendments proposed and enough rubbery chicken eaten to feed Russia for a year. They serve a useful social function as well, in allowing freaks and geeks and strange-o's of all description a bit of convivial interaction and the chance to hold forth on those passionate views that have been burning them up for twelve months. It's almost guaranteed that at least one gigantic row will erupt, involving the relative character merits and demerits of the arguing partners, the training of the past year's U12s and a bag of hurleys that went mysteriously missing. Wildean insults are flung and reputations ruined, while a few teenagers invariably sit in the background, sniggering like Beavis and Butthead.

Then there's always the mad ould loon who doesn't know his arse from the new third-man tackle rule, pontificating like a slightly confused Buddha on everything from the club's chances in the upcoming U21 match (last year's final, naturellement) to the pressing need for a foot spa in the dressing rooms. He really comes into his own during the election of officers, possessing the disconcerting habit of proposing completely inappropriate people for each post. The worst thing about these morons is that they're treated with tremendous respect and deference, and nobody's quite sure why. The last time they saw the inside of the local ground was when the bishop came to bless it in the 1970s, but still people are reticent about shouting, 'For the love of God, shut up! That's the most stupid thing I've heard since your idea last year to coat the goalposts in luminous paint so we could play matches by night. Now sit down or I'll be forced to find new and unpleasant uses for this bolt-tightener.'

The normal pattern then is for one person to blatantly cut across the old geezer, someone else to correct them on their rudeness, a third party to call the second party 'nuttin' but a tramp', and old Buddha to serenely suggest painting an acid-house smiley face in the centre of the pitch to welcome visiting aliens.

This last suggestion is unanimously passed.

ON YOUR MARK

In 1999, the Gaelic Players' Association (GPA) was founded to agitate for better players' rights: extensive medical care, compensation for earnings lost, end-of-season holidays, and so on. Apparently, our inter-county stars had, for decades past, been virtual indentured servants, forced to toil endlessly (at a game they love) for no reward, bar the honour, medals, renown, fun, camaraderie, fitness, cushy jobs in the bank, educational scholarships, sexual favours from young ladies who would, under normal circumstances, be somewhat outside our heroes' range, etc., etc.

This shocking – not to mention appalling – situation could not be allowed to continue, and the GPA nobly dedicated itself to eradicating the association of inequality and exploitation, ultimately creating a veritable utopia for all Gaels, at all levels. Admittedly, they seem to have concentrated primarily on the economic wants of top-level stars thus far, but I'm sure they'll get around to everyone else soon. Probably just been really busy or something.

Their ideology was set out in

THE FIRST MANIFESTO OF THE SOVIET SOCIALIST INTERNATIONAL OF LENINIST/TROTSKYIST/ CUSACKIST SOCIAL AND DEMOCRATIC BROTHER- AND SISTERHOOD OF COMMUNIST TRADE AND FAIR PLAY FROM REFEREES UNION CENTRAL POLITBURO.

Snappy title, eh?

Comrades! A glorious victory has been achieved against the mandarins of capito-fascism and their spineless lackeys! No longer will we watch the fat cats eat all the pie from their swish corporate boxes! Now, they will eat their pie with the rest of us: from the boot of the car!

[Cue crackly brass-band marching music like Lenin used to have them play]

DICTATE 1: Henceforth the GAA will be known as Cumannach Lúthcleas Gael – the Communist Athletic Gaels!

DICTATE 2: We are dedicated to the worldwide overthrow of all amateur voluntary sports bodies. We will then establish the Pan-Global Directorat for Sporting Endeavour.

★

DICTATE 3: All records referring to the association formerly known as the GAA will be destroyed in a symbolic fire in Croker. We might as well chuck in those godawful jerseys Ireland wore in the 2001 International Rules while we're at it.

★

DICTATE 4: And any photos of 1970s hurlers with their hair billowing out from under their helmet. God, those were ghastly.

★

DICTATE 5: The capitalist power-mongers and running-dogs will be given two weeks to hand themselves over voluntarily for torture by our specially trained Wicklow full-backs. If they refuse, roundy bombs with fuses sticking out of them will be thrown into the VIP section of the Hogan at the next big match.

★

DICTATE 6: Competitive sports have been outlawed because they are nothing more than war without the guns … and we only like war with the guns. They have been replaced with gently kicking a ball around in a circle.

DICTATE 7: All teams must wear red jerseys in honour of our great founder, Vladimir Ilyich Cusack. The referee's jersey is a non-issue since all referees have been rounded up and sent to the Monaghan Gulags where they will be forced to try and understand the accent.

DICTATE 8: The national anthem has been abolished. Instead, we will enjoy our new anthem, 'Kill All Rich People (And Anyone Else We Don't Like)'. Soon to be released on Totalitarian Records (CD, LP and MP3 formats).

★

DICTATE 9: Croke Park will be demolished to symbolise the destruction of decadent free-market forces. In its place will be an ugly, grey building with little practical use and no aesthetic value whatsoever. A bit like the Mackey Stand in Limerick.

★

DICTATE 10: All decisions will be made by unaccountable quangos of faceless bureaucrats, whose actions are inexplicable and whose motivations change constantly. So the provincial councils stay.

★

DICTATE 11: The only books available in the GAA Museum (now 'The Record House of the Glorious Revolution') will be *Das Kapital*, that other one Karl Marx wrote and *Babs: A Legend in Irish Sport*. All other literature is forbidden! Severe penalties will be incurred by anyone caught with subversive material like *Communism is Bad, I Preferred Things the Way they Used to Be, I Must Say and Babs: A Legend in Irish Sport*.

★

DICTATE 12: Irish has been replaced by Russian as the primary language of the association. *Dos vedanya, tavarichi Galliki*. For practical purposes, *Sunday Game*-speak will remain the *lingua franca* … at the end of the day.

DICTATE 13: No more cheering is permitted. Supporting one team above another is divisive and bourgeois. It is also enjoyable, and enjoyment has been outlawed too.

★

DICTATE 14: Spreading dirty rumours about teams taking performance-enhancing steroids will cease. This is because performance-enhancing steroids are now mandatory for everyone over the age of five.

★

DICTATE 15: The Scór is now called 'Non-Competitive Exposition of the Musical and Other Talents of Our Comrades Throughout the Association'. The only songs allowed will be our aforementioned anthem, whilst the recitation will be limited to the collected works of Engels. The novelty act has been abolished because laughing is an imperialist act.

★

DICTATE 16: To extend the hand of friendship to our downtrodden brethren overseas, we will invite The Great Satan to play a non-competitive exhibition in the Stalin Dome (formerly known as Semple Stadium). Afterwards, we shall try to poison their president during the presentation by inserting an anthrax-filled needle into the base of the cup.

Players of the world unite! You have nothing to lose but the first round of next year's championship!

Croke is it

Croke Park, of course, is the Mecca of Gaelic games. Everyone knows where it is. Well, everyone except Carlow and Leitrim fans. Everyone has watched a match there. Well, everyone except Carlow and Leitrim fans. And everyone holds this grand old stadium in the fondest regard. Yes, even Carlow and Leitrim fans.

The Jones Road site of the present Croker was opened in 1882 as Butterly's Amusement Park, at which patrons could enjoy such delights as the freak show and bear-baiting. In 1913, the GAA put in a £1,500 down-payment and the next day's papers bemoaned spiralling prices in the property market, claiming, 'Five years ago one could buy a sports ground in Dublin for 2/6 and a handful of toffees.' The grounds were renamed Croke Park. Dr Horatio Spitznagle's Marvellous House of Fun Spectacularium was also considered as a name, but strangely rejected.

The destruction of Dublin during the 1916 Rising had an upside: the rubble was used for building. The famous old terrace was named Hill 16 in honour of that most important of squad members – the first substitute. Construction for the original Cusack Stand began in 1936, though a building strike in 1937 delayed work. Workers' grievances included twenty-five-hour days and being forced to wear flat caps. In 1959, the Hogan Stand was carted off to Limerick and a new one was installed. Other Dublin gifts to Limerick soon followed, like endless suburban sprawl and the wearing of horrible shiny tracksuits.

A new office block for administration, built under the Hogan Stand, was completed in 1982. This made the running of things a whole lot easier, since office work had previously been carried out on the bonnet of someone's car. And, finally, headquarters has now received its greatest facelift – a massive, €200 million, ten-year project that makes Croke Park one of the finest stadiums in the world. All they need now is to change the name back to Butterly's Amusement Park and the circle will be complete.

Famous Rules

– two case studies

I am politically and culturally nationalist, support the promotion of the Irish language and believe in the inviolability of the GAA's amateur status. I also have a third-level education, have lived abroad, enjoy William Gibson's cyberpunk fiction and the artiest of art-house films, and am just about the most socially liberal person you could hope to meet. Seriously – whatever it is, I have no problem with consenting adults doing it.

Which is why I was quite taken aback to be lumped in with 'bigots', 'dinosaurs' and 'conservatives' of all stripes during a divisive and fractious debate which was concluded – though not finally – at the 2005 Congress. I refer, of course, to Rule 42, which excludes certain other sports from GAA pitches, and which has now been put in abeyance during the redevelopment of Lansdowne Road. Though I (reluctantly!) accept the democratic wishes ➔

Grounds for dismissal

– some other stadiums around the country

Semple Stadium, Thurles: Spiritual home of the ancient game, in the town where the association was founded. It's said that true hurling folk kneel in the direction of Semple five times a day to pray.

▷

Páirc Uí Chaoimh, Cork: Renowned for its picturesque setting, excellent sight-lines on the terraces and Ger Canning's mantra-like repetition of 'Down in Cork, they call it the Park' at every available opportunity.

▷

of the majority, I can't describe how galling that decision was for me … and, I suspect, numerous others.

There are many, many reasons why Rule 42 should have been retained. In fact, there are so many that I'd probably need a whole separate book to list them fully. And other writers can, and have, argued its case more persuasively than me (I'm thinking in particular of Donal McAnallen's piece in *High Ball* magazine in May 2001 which forensically addressed and obliterated every single argument for its removal). You all know the pro- and anti-assertions, and have no doubt made your mind up by now.

So I'll limit myself to one, very personal, reason: sheer, cussed stubbornness. Forget all the economic, political or social arguments – I'm just seriously ticked off at the astounding amount of misinformation, machination and plain old deception propounded by those in favour of opening up Croke Park. More astounding still was the way it went virtually unchecked, as legions of – let's be frank here – ill-informed morons trotted out all those old clichés. Such as: the GAA receives more government funding than any other sporting body (really? Let's see the figures); anything funded by the taxpayer belongs to everyone (does this apply to the National Gallery of Ireland, or anyone who received the first-time house buyers' grant?); the GAA is populated by vindictive, exploitative bigots (is this your experience? It ain't mine).

Previous No votes had received a viscerally vicious reaction from various vested interests – a controversy-hungry media, soccer propagandists and the usual rag-tag band of self-hating Uncle Tom figures, among others. Indeed, the breadth and ferocity of the abuse was mindboggling at times. Irish soccer fans, who contemptuously admit that they would not set foot in a GAA ground if their lives depended on it, were still aggrieved enough to engage in ➡

Breffni Park, Cavan: Host to many great Cavan teams and players down the years. Unfortunately, none of them in the past half-century or so.

▷

Gaelic Grounds, Limerick: Has progressed somewhat from the aesthetic horrors of the 1980s and 1990s, but probably still should have sold up to developers and built a spanking new green-field stadium.

▷

sustained tirades against those democratic decisions. In the papers, one random opinion column by a certain culturally enslaved drone described GAA people as braying, drunken loudmouths who had, apparently, strangled at birth other games throughout the country, and the GAA itself as a tinpot organisation which had made a fool of itself across the world. (He also found room to misuse the word 'bigot' in an article concerning Jack Boothman, a Protestant man in a historically Catholic organisation – ho hum.)

The saddest thing was how easily we – GAA people – bended to these bullying tactics. We made wheedling excuses for their intemperance and hostility, and quixotic predictions that, should we extend the hand of friendship, the subsequent positive press would be overwhelming (I'll believe it when I read it). It'd be peace and love and fraternity all the way, brother, though I must admit that sporting ecumenism has never held that much appeal for me. Sure, whatever sports people are *playing* don't matter, as long as they're fit and healthy. But on a broader level, I could never stand those mealy-mouthed 'we're all sports fans' apologists. I mean, to claim to 'like all sports' shows nothing more than a lack of discernment. Hell, I'm obsessed with movies, but I don't unthinkably like all of them. You know, I *make choices*. I'm not a 'sports man', I'm a GAA man; big difference.

Anyway, the inevitable result of all these inter-connecting dynamics was the removal of Rule 42; a sad day, and one I hope won't lead to sadder days in the future. One day, some clever media-theory student will write a dissertation on these events, framing it as an Irish version of Noam Chomsky's *Manufacture of Consent*: living proof that hype can create its own truth, that anything repeated often enough becomes fact. Until then, all us Neanderthal, reactionary troglodytes must grin and bear it. ➜

Casement Park, Belfast: Has suffered its share of upsets, including political (occupation by British army forces), sporting (virtually annual disembowelment by Derry or someone) and sartorial (those migraine-inducing saffron jerseys). ▷

St Tiernach's Park, Clones: Home of the Ulster football final, at least up until swelling crowd numbers made a move to Croke Park inevitable. Cue much gnashing of gold-plated teeth from those poor, put-upon publicans. ▷

It was the root cause of almost as much argument and disorder as the average Ger Loughnane *Sunday Game* appearance, but the Ban actually had solid reasoning to support it. Well, relatively solid in an era when only 2 per cent of the population could vote, and scuttling up chimneys with big brushes was seen as an appropriate activity for ten year olds.

There were two strands to it. The first, prohibiting the playing of or attendance at foreign games, was introduced to counteract the influence of a rival body, the Irish Amateur Athletic Association. It covered sports such as soccer, rugby and tennis, but not, funnily enough, equestrian sports, boxing or basketball. (It was felt that skills in horse-riding and the pugilist arts could come in handy for GAA men during those tricky prison breaks from Van Diemen's Land.) The second part disbarred members of the RIC, British army and assorted other gun-toting hooligans from GAA membership. RIC men had apparently been spying on meetings and reporting to the authorities, the dirty little snitches, so their exclusion was justified.

The Ban was itself banned at the turn of the twentieth century, but reintroduced in the aftermath of a bombastic speech by one T.F. O'Sullivan, who called on Ireland's young blades 'not to ape foreign manners and customs'. T.F. obviously figured that strict Islam, codes of *hara-kiri* or crack-cocaine binges might have detrimental effects on the wholesomeness of the Irish character, and wisely proscribed them.

For decades, congress delegates voted early and voted often on the Ban, which must have gotten pretty boring after fifteen years or so. Though the result remained the same – it stayed – some of the surrounding scenery was of →

Cusack Park, Ennis: Though named after the founder of the GAA, this glorified wrecking yard is, sadly, one of the least impressive grounds in Munster. But it's running neck-and-neck with…

Fraher's Field, Dungarvan: The *dumpo di tutti dumpi*, really. Although, amazingly, it hosted the most successful one-off tournament in GAA history: the 1910 Croke Memorial. So there's mud in my eye.

curiosity value, with delegates sometimes known to defy their voting instructions because of an impassioned speech. At one 1960s Kerry Convention, for example, a motion to remove the Ban met with such aversion that even the proposer and seconder voted against it, which would suggest either an incredibly persuasive anti-rescinding argument or a disturbingly high incidence of split-brain psychosis in Kerry. I'm going with the latter.

In the end, the Ban's demise came with more of a whimper than a bang. At the 1971 congress in Belfast, it was removed from the rulebook without serious dissent. After all those passionate debates and stirring oratories, they just upped and ditched the damn thing. The Ban on RUC and army members playing Gaelic games was also supposed to bite the bullet (pun definitely intended) in 1971, but was withdrawn at a late stage. The issue dragged on to its equally subdued removal, as Rule 21, in 2001, with a PSNI selection even taking on An Garda Síochána the following year.

In the interim, needless to say, certain members of the press had complained long and hard about the supposed 'bigotry' of the Northern counties who had argued for its retention most strongly, decrying them as living in the past and clinging to old prejudices. This, of course, conveniently overlooked such trifling issues as police sectarianism, the harassment and murder of GAA members and the occupation of grounds. The same sages have been noticeably silent since the Ban was fully lifted, despite assurances that doing so would – as with Rule 42 – result in much positive press for the association. Sigh.

In fact, the only time I ever see the Ban mentioned now is when some old garrison games fucker is bemoaning how the GAA stopped him from following his dreams of a career in soccer/rugby/frisbee/whatever. Which automatically makes me want to bring it back. ■

Fitzgerald Stadium, Killarney: A grand pitch, nice location, good sod … and it still only gets a big match every few years. Tough break, Killarney.

Markievicz Park, Sligo: Named after one of the greatest ever Irishwomen and a revolutionary hero. With credentials like that, who cares what the actual ground is like?

Objection,
your honour!

Welcome to the court of Gaelic games, where the long and noble tradition of the objection is held in the high regard it deserves. For as long as there have been sore losers, so there have been objections to results, or even to participation in the first place.

This court is now in session for some of the more memorable ones – all rise.

The case: Tipperary v. Kilkenny, 1900

The objection: Tipperary alleged that five Kilkenny footballers who played them in the All-Ireland semi-final lived in County Tipperary and were not eligible for their rivals.

The verdict: For the plaintiff – who then selected the same five players for the All-Ireland final.

The case: Cork v. Kilkenny, 1905

The objection: Kilkenny objected that Cork's goalkeeper was a reserve in the British army, which was illegal under a 1903 rule.

The verdict: For the plaintiff – replay fixed.

The case: Monaghan v. Cavan, 1915

The objection: After their defeat, Monaghan claimed the crowd had been on the pitch for the last ten minutes, the goalposts were broken, Cavan star Felix McGovern had played for Leitrim and an umpire had saved a certain Monaghan goal three minutes from the end.

The verdict: Nobody had the energy left to give a verdict after sitting through all that evidence.

The case: Limerick v. Dublin, 1925

The objection: Upon losing to Dublin in the very first national hurling league match, the Shannonsiders objected that a Limerick-born member of the Dublin team had played with Croom while at home. Dublin counter-objected.

The verdict: Hung jury – no points for either side.

The case: Kerry v. Cavan v. Kerry, 1925

The objection: After the All-Ireland semi-final, Kerry objected that a Cavan player was living in Mullingar. Cavan counter-objected to a Kerry player who lived in Dublin.

The verdict: Both counties kicked out of the competition.

The case: The GAA v. New York, 1927

The objection: New York won the 'World Championship' by beating Kerry in the Polo Grounds. The GAA here at home objected to the title for some reason or other.

The verdict: Case thrown out.

The case: Clare v. Tipperary, 1938

The objection: Clare objected that Tipp player Jimmy Cooney had been banned under the foreign-games rule when his declaration for the then All-Ireland hurling champions was signed.

The verdict: For the plaintiff – Tipp turfed out of Munster championship.

The case: Kildare v. Meath, 1938

The objection: Kildare objected to a goal scored by Meath after Kildare had stopped playing, thinking the final whistle had blown.

The verdict: Case thrown out – and petulant Kildare withdrew from the GAA for a year in protest.

The case: Antrim v. Kerry, 1946

The objection: Kerry won the All-Ireland semi-final with some – how do I put this? – 'enthusiastic' third-man tackling, and Antrim objected that Kerry had brought the game into disrepute

The verdict: Case thrown out.

The case: Mayo v. Roscommon, 1953

The objection: Mayo objected that Roscommon players, born outside the county, had helped them win the Connacht final.

The verdict: Case thrown out – eventually.

Transfer mart and market

The rules for transfers of players between clubs or counties are intricate and arcane, so much so that one county chairman seriously considered trying to raise the spirit of King Solomon in an attempt to solve a particularly complex *imbroglio* a few years back. (His fellow county-board members haggled him down to the spirit of Michael Landon.)

No one alive actually knows just what, exactly, are the criteria for switching allegiances, but they are believed to include the following: change of address; change in work circumstances; change in educational circumstances; falling out with the manager; falling out with fellow midfielder; snogging fellow midfielder's girl; having to skip town pronto and cash bribes. (Ha! Just kidding about that last one.) All we do know is that at least once a year, someone, somewhere will find themselves in trouble with a disciplinary committee for fielding an improperly registered player. But when teams finally do get the 7,000-page documents in order, thus completing the paperwork, a clever transfer can be a real boon for a team's fortunes. And players have long fled their native soil in the hope of a better life, far away, where fields are greener and there aren't so many bloody others jostling for your position. Several men have won All-Irelands with two counties, such as the unusually named Caleb Crone, who snagged a Celtic Cross with Dublin in 1942 and Cork three years later, despite the considerable handicap of sounding like he should have been burned at the stake for witchcraft in 1660s New England. But I don't suppose he was, if he managed to line out for a match almost three centuries later.

Paul Russell is probably the all-time king of the gadabouts. The Kerry – I think – native played club football in no fewer than eight different counties during a whirlwind career in the 1920s and 1930s, and lined out for the Kingdom and Dublin at inter-county, and Munster and Leinster at inter-provincial. This busy little bee probably found time to represent the Bolshevik Empire in Olympic hammer-throwing while he was at it.

More recently, there has been a raft of high-profile transfers involving big-name stars. And a few nobodies as well. Kildare, of course, became notorious for their 'everybody's welcome' approach during the 1990s, and seemed determined, at one stage, to turn the side into the first GAA version of the Harlem Globetrotters. Karl O'Dwyer joined the Dad from Kerry, Brian Murphy toddled up from Cork and his namesake Lacey nipped over from Tipperary. I also seem to remember Carlow's Garvan Ware transferring to Kildare and then back again within the space of about six months, but may have just dreamt that. Of course, the irony was that the Lilywhites themselves lost two

of their greatest players when Larry Tompkins and Shay Fahey upped sticks for the balmy surrounds of the Lee. But I guess that's conclusive proof that karma exists, which is nice to know.

Others to make that great leap of inter-county faith include uncommonly articulate *Sunday Game* pundit Martin Carney, who played for Donegal and Mayo; Declan Darcy, who nobly agreed to help his dad's county, Leitrim, win something for the first time in ages before returning to help Dublin win absolutely sweet FA; and Kilkenny star Denis Byrne, who enjoyed a brief sojourn with the Tipperary panel in 2003. This was an especially contentious move, given the intense rivalry between these two counties.

Similarly, 'Legend of the Hill'™ Vinnie Murphy played hurling for a little while with Kerry, the Dubs' greatest foes. Still, Vinnie wore that cool 'camouflage'-style helmet when wielding the camán, and that, baby, would make up for anything.

Around the world in eighty games

Gaelic games
have never been more
global than they are now, what
with the easy availability of matches via
satellite and the internet and loads of young professionals travelling
around and setting up clubs because they feel homesick. But it wasn't
always thus.

Oh, my bad – it *was* always thus. In fact, the GAA has a long and
distinguished tradition of adventurous exploits 'out foreign'. So pack
the rucksack, get your shots, root out that old paperback of *The Lord
of the Rings* and prepare to embark on a potted history of Gaelic
games on foreign fields. As they say in only the finest movie trailers,
it's gonna be one hell of a ride…

Europe is our playground

BRITAIN's finest GAA hour, of course, was London's victory over
Cork in the 1901 All-Ireland hurling final. Jaysus – try explaining that
one to angry delegates at the county board AGM. Glasgow, believe it
or not, got in on the act by beating Antrim in the 1910 quarter-final,
though rumours persisted that the feared local 'kiss' played a big part
in the victory. Farther south, meanwhile, Hertfordshire has its catchment

area in posh places like Buckinghamshire, and didn't once feature a young Jeffrey Archer in goals at U16 level.

Hopping into a nippy speedboat for a quick digression, the **CHANNEL ISLANDS** of Guernsey and Jersey have both formed clubs. While not exactly setting the world on fire thus far, the inclusion of Jim Bergerac in the panel is hoped to be the catalyst for greater success. Although you'd imagine Lovejoy might add greater heft to the midfield. Or even Ray off *Minder*.

GERMANY's Dusseldorf club was founded in 1992 and went on to win every competition they entered, as the Germans are wont to do. (Nah, only joking.) Go west a bit and, in 1910, Cork and Tipperary played exhibition matches in **BELGIUM**, but the tour was a disaster, with negligible attendances. One of the party ruefully remarked, 'And I thought the Railway Cup was bad.'

The Hague in **HOLLAND** is living proof that the EU is good for more than just giving lots of money to farmers. GAA has been played in this bureaucratic city since the 1970s. And speaking of **LUXEMBOURG** (even though we weren't), The Seventh Most Pointless Country on the Planet has also contributed to the worldwide spread of our national games by hosting Europe's longest-running tournament, the Black Stuff Sevens, and Poc Fada na hEorpa.

Paris, **FRANCE** (as opposed to Paris, Texas) is the home of the Eiffel Tower, cyclists in stripy sweaters and beautiful women who pout a lot, but it's also the home of Paris Gaels, the first affiliated club on the continent and instrumental in the establishment of a European Board. *Zut alors*! (GAA activities in Paris, Texas, are unknown at time of writing.)

I've seen the rain fall in Africa

Irish UN soldiers organised their own tournaments in the **CONGO** during the 1960s. A 'Railway Cup' final was even held, but had to be abandoned after then-UN observer in the Congo, Conor Cruise O'Brien, rushed onto the pitch, foaming at the mouth about pan-nationalism and Sinn Féin and all that.

Occasional hurling matches used take place in **SOUTH AFRICA** among workers in engineering firms, like Environmentally Unfriendly Power Stations 'R' Us. Bizarrely, Tuam Krugers, founded in the County Galway town in 1900, were actually named after the President of the Boer Republic, proving that political correctness hadn't spread as far as the West of Ireland at that time. Or any time, really.

Staying in Africa, but veering off a bit to go into the Middle East, the Almarai Milk Cup was held in 1985 on the endless sandy expanse that is **SAUDI ARABIA**. A company called Masstock provided the hurlers. Allah guaranteed the fruits of victory. Meanwhile, the Dubai Sevens has been played since 1994, cleverly combining Gaelic fun and frolics with some grade A duty-free shopping. Bring me back a carton of smokes, will ya?

I come from a land down under

The first reference to hurling in **AUSTRALIA** dates from 1850, with the game recorded in places like the interestingly named Port Fairy (I shudder to think what sailors used to get up to there after six months at sea). A fall-off in emigration to Oz threatened GAA there in the 1960s, but fortunately the 1980s rode to the rescue with a crippling decade-long recession.

Okay by me in America

The **UNITED STATES OF AMERICA'S** illustrious history didn't look so illustrious at the beginning, when an ill-fated party travelled from Ireland in 1888 and seventeen never returned. Holy disappearing players! Things rapidly improved, however, and soon there were tons of clubs and intercontinental tournaments (to go with the intercontinental ballistic missiles stored at the back of the Old Stand). New York is probably the most successful Yankee team, winning the football league three times and competing in the Connacht championship alongside all the other weird teams like North Yorkshire, the Antarctic and Leitrim.

Branches of the GAA were founded in the Big Apple in 1891, with predictable names like Brooklyn Wolfe Tones. It would have been much funnier if they'd been called Coney Island Hot-Dog Guzzlers or Queens in Their Tiaras. The 1947 All-Ireland final, of course, was played in the Polo Grounds baseball stadium. Plans to bring next year's World Series to Fraher's Field in Dungarvan are said to be still at the discussion stage.

Leaping onto our high-powered scooters and, like, scooting down the American land mass, we come to **ARGENTINA**. The Buenos Aires hurling club was founded in 1900, but while a worldwide scarcity of ash during World War II killed off the sport there (this is actually true, I swear), an area of Buenos Aires called Hurlingham exists to this day. Which is so bizarre, it doesn't bear thinking about.

Go east young man

The Asian Gaelic Games Tournament has been running for over a decade now. Around 400 ex-pats travel from all over the mightiest of continents to participate in its largest amateur sporting event. Though I would expect the Punjabi Snake-Handling Championships to run it a close second. Named in honour of the late Derek Brady, one of the founders, the tournament welcomes players from such exotic locales as China, Japan, Korea, Singapore, Vietnam and the Midlands counties.

To spice it up a bit for next year, could I suggest corralling everyone onto a mysterious island controlled by a malevolent opium trader, à la the most formulaic of kung-fu flicks, and letting them fight to the death in a frenzy of blood, fists and madness? Sure, for the Midlands lads, it'll be like they never left home. ■

Maybe it's becawse Oi'm a Lahndahnaaaahh...

...that I really want to see London do well. And here's five famous Cockernees who could make a difference to their fortunes.

Reggie Kray: Tough, ruthless, prepared to do anything to get results ... the perfect inter-county manager. 'Cept for the fact that he's dead, of course.

Babs Windsor: Former *Carry On* star's bubbly personality and cheeky grin would distract the opposition defence.

Michael Caine: Could confuse his marker by repeatedly intoning, 'D'you know summink? Not a lotta people know that' in his distinctive monotone.

Brett Anderson: Snake-hipped former Suede frontman is tall, has a good sidestep and knows lots of lovely sailor boys who'd make solid corner-backs.

Ken Livingstone: Red Ken could, in his capacity as Mayor of London, divert 90 per cent of city funds to the building of training facilities and extend the Tube to Croke Park.

The female of the species

Rising attendances, higher profiles, improving standards, more representation in administration and the media, the fastest-growing sport in Ireland … and thankfully, no longer restricted to just washing dirty jerseys or making tea.

Women's place in the GAA has truly arrived, though I must scotch the unjust perception that they were, until very recently, second-class citizens in the association. (A state of affairs not helped, I admit, by that crack about washing jerseys.) Sure, women's sports may not have been fully respected for a long time, but this was no more than representative of the patriarchy inherent in Irish society as a whole. This was a man's world – a *man's* man's world, by God – and like with jury duty, contraception and equitable representation, women drew the short straw.

But, historically, the GAA was surprisingly forward thinking and egalitarian. Camogie, organised now for over a century, was quite radical in its way, allowing a fair degree of female independence at a time when the notion of women playing sport was almost universally frowned upon. I can recall standing on terraces twenty years ago with my sisters, while my mam sat in the stands (the same sisters also played camogie in school). Women were always involved at club level, doing unglamorous but important jobs in areas like administration, fundraising and transport – and, in my mother's case, nursing split heads at juvenile hurling matches. And I don't believe women ever felt unwelcome or threatened whilst attending a match, in contrast to the feral atmosphere generated by hordes of aggressive soccer fans.

I also have fond memories of unisex childhood hurling teams, when 'girl power' meant sledging with the best of them. The fairer sex played a crucial role as part of that grand old tradition – the girl on the boys' team. When I was growing up, we always had several girls on our teams. Bloody good they were, too. My father, ever devoted to throwing a big lump of a rock through the glass ceiling, gave starting positions to girls way before it became fashionable. Hell, this was before it even became fashionable for women to be let out of the kitchen. Whether this was due to small player pools or a heartfelt desire to balance the gender scales, I don't know, though I always suspected that the motive may have been more practical – they were better players.

Up to about U14, girls are physically bigger, stronger and better balanced than boys (being that gangly can't be good for our co-ordination). They're also mentally bigger, stronger and better balanced, and emotionally and socially too. Add the fact that their skill levels are just as good as their male counterparts, ergo girls make equal, if not better, players. My pops knew that, which explains why I played on tons of teams featuring girls. The greatest hour for juvenile feminism in my area came in the 1983–84 local primary schools B hurling final, when our beloved alma mater made history, and the pages of the regional press, by playing six girls in the first fifteen – and in central positions.

This policy led to some funny moments. Once, when playing a crowd of gougers whose parish I can't legally name here, one of the opposition tried to needle his marker (a girl) by hitting her. He probably hadn't expected that she would just get angry and start walloping back. Such was the beating our wannabe Xena dished out that I actually think the kid started crying, putting something of a dent in his hard-man image. Served him right.

Having a girl on the team was so commonplace, in fact, that for years I thought it was mandatory, like arriving at the match on time. Of course, as time passed, we gradually noticed slight, but critical, differences beginning to emerge between us, so the career of our unisex team drew to a close. But I'll always have fond memories of those times – male and female together, working in unison toward a common cause: victory, the pursuit of excellence and beating the lard out of anyone who played dirty. Rock on, sisters.

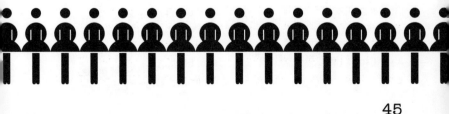

'BUT WHERE DOES ALL THE MONEY GO!?'

This, painfully, is one of the most common screeches heard from the large anti-GAA faction in this benighted land (right up there with such inanities as 'They won't let Protestants play' and 'Croke Park rightfully belongs to the taxpayers').

Every big match is now marked by screaming banner headlines which invariably place great emphasis on the amount of money accrued from the previous day's action. 'Bumper payday for the GAA!' has become the mantra of the lazy and the tragically retarded. If the game was a draw, even better: now one can jabber on about 'another money-spinner for Croke Park' and joke that the draw had been engineered by avaricious GAA mandarins. But why is this obsession with gate receipts limited to Gaelic games? Where are the subtly snide comments about financial windfalls when 45,000 rugby supporters pay top dollar to watch the national team? Or the suggestion that drawn FAI Cup matches are contrived by Merrion Square to squeeze more shillings from the punters?

All this nonsense leads to others smelling blood and asking – nay, *demanding* to know – how the money is divvied up, as if they had some sort of stake in it. To the uninformed, the vast bulk of revenue goes straight into some Gaelic version of an Ansbacher account, squirreled away by the Croke

Park *politburo* for future venal purposes. This, despite the fact that the association publishes full accounts each year and, indeed, has been commended by the Irish auditors' body for fiscal clarity and transparency.

The correct response to such unmannerly intrusiveness is, of course, to extend one's middle finger, waggle it about and laugh, 'That's where it goes. See? Me flipping you the bird is where the money goes. Want a closer look at my 'accounts'?' But we are generous, tolerant people, so if they really, *really* want to know, just direct them towards the huge amounts of hard cash invested in teams, grounds, administration, coaching and promotion, through local and national frameworks every year.

Actually, make it even simpler: turn them in the direction of their nearest spanking GAA grounds and tell 'em to keep walking until they get tangled up in the goal nets. (Just don't mention the free house extensions, vibrating massage chairs, bottles of thirty-year-old cognac, Semtex stashes for the imminent resumption of the armed struggle, etc., etc.)

Pros and cons

Constant references to financial windfalls for the GAA have inevitably led to increased talk about payment for players. It's almost become a *Sunday Game* ritual for the pundits to throw out the usual, vaguely mindless bunkum about 'giving the players a few bob' (though interestingly, I have yet to hear these ideas expanded upon with any sort of concrete, workable proposal). After all, the experts argue, these are the people who bring in the money, apparently making intolerable sacrifices along the way; should they not get a nice big slice of the pie? **Well, no, frankly. And here's why.** ➡

1. Ireland is a small country and the population doesn't exist to support professionalism in Gaelic games. Professional rugby and soccer clubs are already struggling to survive.

2. If inter-county players are paid, should equally dedicated club players not receive recompense? And should inter-county players be paid when representing their club or college?

3. Managers, groundsmen, youth trainers, bus drivers, administrators and everyone else who volunteers at club or county level should also be paid, since many invest just as much time and effort as top players.

4. It's impossible to define at what age payment should begin. Should inter-county minors, many of whom are still in school, be paid? And what about U21, junior and intermediate?

5. The issue of taxation hasn't even been mentioned yet. Is this payment to be taxed? And should all the freebies players currently get also be taxed as the earnings of a professional?

6. Nobody is forced to play inter-county. People choose to play because it's a social outlet, keeps them healthy and, fundamentally, they enjoy it. Should everyone get paid for engaging in their hobby?

7. For every self-employed player who loses out on overtime, several are nudged to the top of the employment queue by GAA connections or by the relative measure of fame accrued.

8. There are many commercial opportunities for players in the form of endorsements, boot deals, personal appearances, etc.

9. Does every single thing we do in this lousy world have to have a financial reward? The feeling of pride and satisfaction at winning an All-Ireland or other major title can't be measured in monetary terms.

10. And finally – if you feel aggrieved that soccer stars and tennis players can earn a fortune from playing their game and you can't, *go take up one of those sports!*

The games

Diamonds
and hurls

◆◆◆◆◆◆◆

It's been heralded as the true Irish art form. It's been called the gentlemen's game for gentlemen. It's been described as the soul of the nation in sporting form. It's even been labelled 'the *Riverdance* of sport', but we'll quickly gloss over that one.

Hurling must suffer a world of pretentiousness, aggrandisement and plain old *ráiméis* being thrown at it, but there is substance beneath the sheen. Look behind all the melodramatic descriptions and hokey mythologising, and the fact remains that it is probably the finest field sport in the world, with combinations of technical adroitness, timing, nerve and flair sometimes reaching wondrous levels. Even for a mediocre mullocker like myself, the odd moment of magic, of stepping momentarily into a more exquisite realm of the self, was possible. Hurling is a gem of a sport, and we're lucky to have it.

Of course, that's not to say the beautiful game is without its faults. First off, it's never really caught on beyond the traditional agricultural parts of the country. Hurling has fallen into disrepair in formally healthy areas like Laois and the Ulster counties, while Kerry and Roscommon don't even compete at the top level any more. The Leinster championship has become a pathetic cakewalk for Kilkenny, and hurling is played seriously in only a third of the counties devoted to football. The last eight All-Irelands have been won by the traditional Big Three, with Cork and the Cats sharing all but one of those. Furthermore, football has come to overshadow the small ball game, primarily because of the outstanding success of the back-door qualifying system.

But hurling has been in worse trouble before. At least now, at the beginning of the year, a good seven or eight counties have some hope of winning the All-Ireland, with five or six pretty confident of their chances. Two decades ago, a few counties dominated the scene; everyone else was cannon fodder. The success of former minnows like Clare and Offaly has had an irreversibly positive effect, in that almost any county can now believe that unprecedented improvement is a possibility; and, with the right application and self-belief, a probability. The days when Cork, Tipp and Kilkenny expected to beat all opponents – and those opponents expected to get beaten – are, thankfully, long buried.

Anyway, you mightn't know this, but I am legally bound to follow the dictates of writing on hurling, long established through custom and practice, which decree that all articles must feature several blurry reminiscences, numerous moments of sentimentality and at least one or two obviously made-up incidents. With that in mind, here are the standout memories of my lifetime watching and playing the game.

1982: Kilkenny hammered Cork in the first All-Ireland final I attended. I remember Christy Heffernan rampaging through for two goals, and the disappointment of two young Cork lads nearby, expressed in the time-honoured practice of scratching their names into the concrete with a piece of broken glass.

ALSO 1982: Two players from my home club won All-Ireland minor medals.

1984: My primary school reached the final of the local competition for the first time in, ooh, ages. We lost, but it was great to be there.

1985: Lost the final again, this time as captain. I blame the fact that the final episode of classic/rubbish sci-fi series *V* was broadcast the night before, thus disturbing my preparations.

1987: Richard Stakelum made his much-imitated but never equalled 'the famine is over' speech before 45,000 people in Killarney's Fitzgerald Stadium.

ALSO 1987: After receiving a blow to the hand in a divisional semi-final, I returned home to watch long-forgotten Peter Cushing flick *The Creeping Flesh*, and became convinced that the darkening bruise on my hand and the unfolding events on screen were somehow inextricably linked. I passed out just as the reawakened prehistoric monster-man, on the rampage around some unconvincing sets depicting Victorian London, began tearing the face off an upper-class

- - - - - - - - - - - - - - - -

Poc-ker up

Five interesting factoids about hurling's spin-off competition, the Poc Fada.

1.

It's based on the ancient saga the Táin Bó Cuailgne, in which Setanta drove a sliotar over the mountains between Louth and Armagh. Or so *he* claimed.

sleazeball with sadistic sexual peccadilloes. (I'm not kidding. This really happened.)

1990: Kilkenny and Offaly's Leinster semi was watched by a tiny crowd, with everyone else plumping for the horrors of Ireland v. Egypt in the soccer World Cup. They said this marked the end of the GAA's ascendancy. They were wrong.

1991: My last game as a player. I didn't do too well, but caught one ball on the double just right and drove it seventy yards down the field. Pretty sweet.

ALSO 1991: My brother won an All-Ireland junior medal.

1995: Clare won the All-Ireland for the first time in about a billion years and I watched it all from behind the bar in a hotel in Lisdoonvarna. (Didn't wear the straw hat, though.) Yeeeaa-hoo-hoo-hooo!!

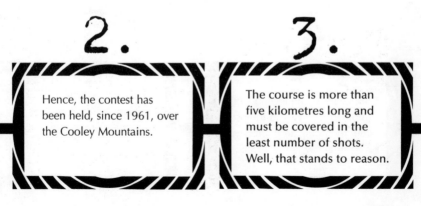

2.

Hence, the contest has been held, since 1961, over the Cooley Mountains.

3.

The course is more than five kilometres long and must be covered in the least number of shots. Well, that stands to reason.

1997: The backdoor was introduced and a revitalised championship got yet another shot in the arm.

ALSO 1997: I emigrated for the first and only time in my life, three days after a great All-Ireland final between Clare and Tipp – later immortalised in verse form by Paul Durcan (the final, not my move to Japan).

2000: I took a walk inside an empty, and newly renovated, Croke Park. I swear to God, it felt like a temple, with the promise of future epics whispered on the breeze. Better stop now before I get all embarrassed.

2004: I followed one of those epics, the Munster final between Waterford and Cork, via frantic text messages to a Thai-Irish bar in Bangkok. Must say, I think I prefer *The Sunday Game*, all told.

(Hi, just checking – have I mentioned meat teas and Tom Semple's field at all in there?)

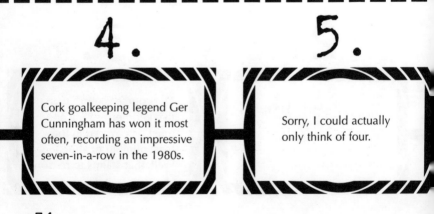

4.

Cork goalkeeping legend Ger Cunningham has won it most often, recording an impressive seven-in-a-row in the 1980s.

5.

Sorry, I could actually only think of four.

Playing footsie

It may not have the historical pedigree or artistic purity of hurling, nor can it draw on mythical iconography for promotional purposes. Some people even debate whether or not it's even, technically, an Irish game. But there is no doubt that Gaelic football is this nation's number one sport, in terms of crowds, TV audiences, organised competition and the ferocious grip it exerts on the public imagination for four months each year. Hurling is like those delicate, beautifully crafted novels the big publishing houses put out to make themselves feel like they're doing something for the love of art. Football, on the other hand, is the guaranteed bestseller, the blockbuster, the rock upon which the whole endeavour is built. This is the money-maker.

Thankfully, the past few years have seen, in tandem with ever-increasing interest, a startling upturn in quality and quantity in the inter-county game. The 2005 championship, for instance, was one of the greatest in anyone's memory, with the drawn Dublin–Tyrone quarter-final, in particular, a purist's delight. The following year, the Dubs served up another all-time classic against Mayo, which even prompted the notorious grumps on the *Sunday Game* panel to metaphorically kneel and pay homage. For anyone who remembered the dark days of the late 1980s – when Connacht and Ulster regularly got creamed on reaching Croke Park; when All-Ireland finals invariably descended into messy wars of attrition; when scores were low, whole seasons were horrendously boring and shorts were almost illegally tight – it must have seemed like some sort of wonderful dream.

Of course, there had been previous golden ages for football. Certainly when I was a little tyke, it was the *ichi-ban*, number one, blue-eyed boy of the association, with 350,000 people crammed into Croker to watch the All-Ireland (and several more floating about in the Royal Canal, listening to the cheers). Kerry and Dublin's epic sagas of the 1970s didn't just capture the sporting public's interest – they wined it, dined it, and bought it two dozen red roses and a Ferrero Rocher. And the Kingdom's legendary bid for five-in-a-row in 1982 whisked it away for a shotgun marriage on a beach in the Cayman Islands. It was like Mills & Boon with studs on, and even manlier jawlines.

But then, alas, *après le deluge*... The romance died, with nothing but a messy divorce and crippling alimony payments to show for it. Declining quality, increased cynicism and the fact that only about two-and-a-half teams were likely to win in any given year resulted in a deep depression for inter-county football, though it obviously continued to thrive at club level. For me, the nadir was reached with Meath's brutalisation of Cork in 1988, when actually kicking the ball and stuff seemed less important than a murderous win-at-all-costs attitude, and a facility and taste for GBH. Now, though we get the odd on-field ruckus still, those medieval days seem well behind us (as one would rightly expect from something medieval).

Obviously, however, further improvements are possible. Call me a sentimental sap, but I'd like to see a return to the old skool. The catch-and-kick, booted-pass style of football is much more

pleasing to the eye than these never-ending chains of short fisted passes. Which would you rather see: six super-fit androids buzzing around in ever-decreasing circles of hand passes, or some creative genius like Ciaran McDonald or Gooch catching the ball, taking a quick look and totally changing the direction of play with a sliced foot pass of sixty yards?

Now, I understand that winning is everything, and sod art. So if victory can be guaranteed by avoiding any contact with the ball at all and spending the seventy minutes doing push-ups and humping bags of coal up and down the terraces, then that's what teams are going to do. I'd just like to point out that recent All-Ireland winners have, almost without exception, been among the top two or three most skilled and most entertaining teams in the country. Just look at the game's name – after all the sports science and psychology, the tactics and conditioning, there's still a ball and you've still got to kick it.

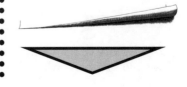

Pay attention – here comes the history part

Anyone suspicious that football receives more attention and tender loving care than hurling may be interested to learn that, as far back as 1527, the Statutes of Galway actually banned the latter: 'No time to use nor occupy the hurlinge of the little ball … but only the great football.' A banning? That seems unfair. And sure, how are we supposed to get young fellas interested if they're liable to be hanged, drawn and quartered for playing the game… [*repeat to fade*]

Before the foundation of the GAA, a football-esque game called Caid was played in Kerry, wherein

Let's see you do that again

Some of the most memorable – but in a peculiar sort of way – scores that I could come up with in five minutes of *really* hard thinking.

Football

2002, FIONÁN MURRAY (Cork): An overhead kicked goal which would have done justice to Pelé.

2001, JOE KAVANAGH (Cork): Maradona-esque dribble through the defence to finish with a green flag.

2000, MARTIN DALY (Clare): Ingeniously back-heeled a point while surrounded by defenders.

1998, SOME GUY WHOSE NAME ESCAPES ME (Erin's Isle): A ridiculously bendy shot which hit both posts and bounced back out, but was adjudged to have crossed the line somewhere in the middle.

1996, COLM COYLE (Meath): Long, long, *loooong* kick that bounced about twenty yards from goal and over the bar to earn an improbable (and typically jammy) draw for Meath.

1983, JOE McNALLY (Dublin): Let the ball run through his legs, then flicked it with the inside of his heel to the net.

1983, BARNEY ROCK (Dublin): Grabbed a misplaced kick-out around forty yards from goal and promptly lobbed it back in over the goalie's head.

1978, MIKEY SHEEHY (Kerry): You know the one I'm talking about.

Hurling

2005, EOIN KELLY (Tipperary): Ran onto a loose ball to rise, spin and shoot over without looking at the posts.

2005, NIALL HEALY (Galway): Kicked soccer-style past the Kilkenny goalie.

2001, KEVIN BRODERICK (Galway): Danced around the defence like a cheeky urchin from *Oliver!*, before impudently lifting the sliotar over Eamon Kennedy's head and finishing with a point.

2001, RORY McCARTHY (Wexford): Leaped into the air and connected beautifully to flick into the net.

1993, D.J. CAREY (Kilkenny): Volleyed home with the stick after his own shot had been saved.

1992, TOMÁS MULCAHY (Cork): Displayed all the skills of tennis, juggling and sprinting to produce a unique, if legally questionable, goal against Limerick.

1987, NICKY ENGLISH (Tipperary): Lost his hurley but controlled and dribbled the ball, like Cruyff in his pomp, before side-footing home for a famous goal.

1983, JIMMY BARRY MURPHY (Cork): A stunning overhead double, on a long John Fenton delivery, which happened so fast nearly everybody missed it.

a leather ball was forced from parish to parish by massed groups of men. Ironically, this is exactly what most irks Kerry folk about football nowadays, particularly when the forcing is being done by massed groups of inexhaustible Ulstermen.

In the eighteenth century, football matches in Kildare, Meath and Dublin were mentioned in the papers, with one John Dunton reporting, rather effetely, that in Fingal 'the people trip and shoulder very handsomely'. Sounds more like a *Pride and Prejudice*-style square dance than a typical Dublin derby, but anyway…

If you've been labouring under the misapprehension that football is pure and unsullied compared to heinous English games, think again: in the early years of the association, ground football was predominant, and kicking from the hand was unknown. And it gets worse – phalanxes of backs and forwards engaged each other in scrimmages. Rugger *and* soccer influences? Excuse me while I spin in my grave for a little while.

59

Me darlin' dual

Brian Murphy may not be a name that instantly stands out – indeed, if you live in Cork, you're probably sitting next to a Brian Murphy right now – but the Nemo Rangers man has achieved something nobody else in the GAA's history ever has, or probably ever will. Between 1969 and 1981, Murphy completed the full set of inter-county medals: minor, U21 and senior, in hurling and football, with All-Stars and Railway Cups in both thrown in for good measure. Oh, and four club football All-Irelands too.

Holy *shit*. Now that's what I call a busy social life.

Welcome to the wonderful world of dual stars, a group which may – if the doomsayers are correct – be in terminal decline. A bit like the giant panda. Certainly, the numbers representing their county in the two games seem to be smaller now, though most play both for the club or college. But I guess the ever-increasing squeeze on players' time and resources – more training, more intensity in training, more time battling rush-hour traffic to get to training, more pressure from panic-stricken, unsuccessful managers to choose just one game – will eventually ensure their demise.

It will be a sad day when the last dual player rides off into the sunset, saddlebags laden down with a hurley, a pair of football gloves and several medals in both, because there have been some storied practitioners of this noble art down the years. Most of them, annoyingly enough, from Cork.

Teddy McCarthy, of course, made history in 1990 as the only man to win two All-Ireland senior medals in the one year on the field of play. His comrade Denis Walsh was dropped for the football final. Yee-*owch*. **Dual rating:** a real gem.

Jimmy Barry Murphy has a raft of medals and awards from both codes, making him just about the most honoured dual star of all time. **Dual rating:** sparkling.

 Though even he couldn't match **Ray Cummins'** record of eleven consecutive senior provincial medals from 1969 to 1979. *And* he made the Team of the Millennium. **Dual rating:** eleven carat.

 Though even he, in turn, couldn't match **Jack Lynch's** famous six Celtic Crosses in a row, from 1941 to 1946. He later earned renown, I believe, as a public figure of some sort. **Dual rating:** priceless.

 Though none of them could match the aforementioned **Brian Murphy**, really, when you think about it. **Dual rating:** what a pearl.

 William J. Spain was the first to win All-Irelands in both codes, and did so with two different teams. In 1887, he was a member of the Limerick side that won the first ever football All-Ireland (bizarrely enough) and, in 1889, lined out for Dublin as they captured the hurling (bizarrely enough squared). **Dual rating:** a valuable antique.

In 1982, Offaly's **Liam Currams** became one of the few modern dual All-Ireland winners, following his hurling win the previous year. **Dual rating:** diamond geezer.

Cam' on everybody

Women really did have it tough back in the bad old good old days, didn't they? I mean, not only were they denied the vote, weren't allowed work and had to wear whalebone corsets, but the pioneers of camogie – the women of a Dublin branch of the Gaelic League – had to conceal their hurleys under long dust-coats on the way to practice. I suppose their self-righteous and astronomically uptight fathers would not have approved of such an unbecoming carry-on. The morons.

(Tragically, couture-related problems continued to dog the game. The hobble skirts in vogue during the early days lived up to their name by, yep, hobbling the players' movement, and, until 1972, teams competed in an utterly unsuitable outfit of a loose-fitting tunic and blouse. They were then lumbered with those awful-looking pleated skirt things, and even in the present day compete in some sort of cross between a skirt and shorts called, oddly enough, a 'skort'. I'm sorry if I appear a little obsessed with this, but it's really annoying. Why don't they just wear shorts and jerseys like everyone else!?)

Anyway, the doughty ladies of the Keating branch persisted, and a public demonstration of camogie was arranged in 1904. A set of rules for a twelve-a-side game was subsequently drawn up. The name, by the way, comes from the word camóg, a less widely used term for camán in old writings.

Camogie celebrated its centenary in 2004, but despite its longevity, it never seems to have caught on in the way, say, women's football is now doing. I understand that the hype and exposure surrounding sport have ballooned over the decades – and nowadays women are more encouraged to partake in physical exertions that don't involve sweeping the floor or juggling two toddlers, a mixing bowl and a poorly family pet – but it's an unhealthy statistic that a mere seven counties have ever won the All-Ireland senior championship, and two of those only within the last decade or so. Dublin, Cork and, to

Noteworthy moments in camogie history

1900: The controlling body, Cumann Camógaíochta na hÉireann, was established, though it experienced some difficulties, being refounded in 1911 and 1923, briefly splitting in 1924 and finally holding its first congress in 1925. But they do say women take ages to get ready.

1912: Dublin beat Louth in the first inter-county match.

a lesser extent, Kilkenny have dominated camogie in a way unparalleled even by hurling's Big Three, or Kerry and Dublin in football. Between 1942 and 1961 one woman, Dublin's Kathleen Mills, captured as many All-Irelands (fifteen) as the remaining four winning counties combined.

As with hurling, the inherent difficulty of the game is probably the main reason why it has never been overly competitive at the top level and seems in a constant struggle for participatory numbers. Though immensely rewarding when done properly, the problem with camogie is that it's damn hard to do properly. And while the current Cork and Tipperary sides, for instance, contain players who wouldn't look out of place on men's teams of any standard, they are streets ahead of their (relatively few) competitors. Still, it's not all gloom, since player participation, particularly at juvenile level, is quite healthy, which really is the whole point of organising sport.

And the recent emergence of Tipperary, Wexford, Galway and Limerick at senior level will, with luck, see a more keenly contested All-Ireland in the near future. It's also good to see greater administrative coalescence with the GAA.

Maybe camogie is the sort of sport about which we will constantly fret, panicked that its limited geographical spread and demanding skills will mean an inevitable demise. And maybe, like hurling, it will continue to confound our expectations. Here's hoping – a hundred years of history shouldn't be tossed away lightly. ■

1915: The first competition, the Ashbourne Cup for universities, was held. The trophy was named after the bumptious-sounding Lord Ashbourne who, despite the 'Lord of the Raj' type name, was actually a big cheese in the Gaelic League.

1922: During the revitalised Tailteann Games, camogie was played from five to seven each evening. Then the girls were hurried home to change into a nice frock for supper while the chaps drank brandy and discussed the situation in the Belgian Congo.

A woman's world

A few years ago, an RTÉ radio programme found itself embroiled in controversy when some clown trashed women's football as pointless, of very poor quality and 'an excuse for silly women to lose some weight'. The reaction was vehement, with the caller quickly denounced as the unreconstructed cave-troll he so clearly was. Shortly afterwards, there was a similar incident, in the aftermath of the All-Ireland final, when an *Irish Times* letter-writer expressed his disapproval of these unladylike activities in Croke Park. This sport, he declared, was unsuitable for young women's bodies, since it could cause bruises and knocks and all sorts of nasty things like that. Again, the correspondent was given short, indeed brutal, shrift.

These incidents demonstrated two things: that the famed 'male chauvinist pig', sadly, still existed; and that women's football was being taken increasingly seriously by the majority. Founded as recently as 1974, the sport has improved in standard all the time, and is now firmly established as a valid unit of the GAA as a whole. It is also said to be the fastest-growing game in Ireland, male or female, which is amazing in some ways – a sporting version of a Velvet Revolution. Like a cult album gradually taking hold of music lovers' imaginations through word of mouth, women's football has attracted tens of thousands of devotees

1932: Dublin beat Galway in the first All-Ireland final.

1942: The All-Ireland final was broadcast on radio for the first time.

1948: From 1948 until 1966, Dublin enjoyed the longest winning streak in the history of Gaelic games, capturing eighteen out of nineteen senior All-Irelands. Beat that, Pat Spillane and co.

while hardly registering on the public radar. Some recent All-Ireland final crowds have neared 35,000, which dwarfs such final attendances as the FAI cup or women's soccer world cup.

There are a few obvious contributory factors. The sport itself is attractive, for both players and spectators, defined by good, crisp football and a welcome lack of the negativity and abrasive physicality which have become prevalent in the men's game. It's an open, entertaining brand of play, with less fouling and more actual football. The finals have been played at Croke Park since 1986, and the first to be televised live, the thrilling draw and replay between Monaghan and Waterford in 1998, also whetted the public's appetite for this fledgling sport. There has been a healthy spread of winners since then, with Laois, Mayo, Waterford, Galway and Cork all capturing the crown. And such innovations as the countdown clock and full-time hooter mark the organisation as forward-thinking and imaginative.

In one sense, I feel the burgeoning popularity of women's football is a bad thing, because it will, in all likelihood, draw young girls away from playing camogie. But then I think, what the hell – that's for the camogie people to sort out. After all, football is another sport we are dedicated to promoting, and the women's game is doing its share, with national championships at all age levels, inter-provincial, university and club competitions, and primary schools leagues organised by Cumann na mBunscol. The sport is also indulging its *wanderlust*, with clubs and tournaments springing up around the world, while annual All-Stars selections honour the finest individual performers.

I just have one teensy little quibble. Is there any chance that the official name of the game might be changed from *ladies'* football? 'Lady' seems such an old-fashioned word in this context, so twee it's almost patronising. What's wrong with 'women's football', as I've been using? After all, it's a woman's world – the rest of us just live in it.

1983: Castleisland player Mary Geaney, later secretary of the Kerry camogie board, was goalkeeper in the Irish hockey team that won the intercontinental cup in Kuala Lumpur. A place which, unlike Castleisland, I've actually been to.

1998: The All-Ireland final was first televised live, with Cork beating Galway.

1999: All competitions were henceforth played by fifteen-a-side teams on full-size pitches.

Talk to the hand!

It's funny how fashions change and things go out of favour, for no other reason than that they do. When I was growing up, for instance, handball was quite a popular little game, with television coverage of the All-Ireland finals and almost every parish possessing its own alley. Cut to about ten years later, and the only activities to be witnessed in many of those alleys were tramps bushy drinking, kids snogging and the glacially slow growth of various strains of weed.

I don't know why handball became uncool and passé, because in many ways it's the perfect sport for an increasingly urbanised world. All you need are three concrete walls, some markings on the ground and a rubber ball. It's cheap, accessible, relatively easy to master, and the alley could double as a handy venue for gang rumbles or aspiring graffiti artists. What more could you ask of a community facility? But for some reason, over the decades, 'the yoot' seems to have discarded handball for such delights as skateboarding, basketball and cutting me off in the queue for cigarettes down the newsagents.

Which is a pity, because handball has a fascinating history. The game has long been played here, with courts dating back to the eighteenth century. Even more impressively, some scholars have linked Irish handball to such diverse locales in the space-time continuum as Imperial Rome and medieval England. In 1788, the colourfully named Thomas 'Buck' Whaley won a hundred sovereigns playing handball in Jerusalem, no less. After the 1798 Rebellion, it is claimed, the United Irishmen held meetings in ballcourts. And I'm pretty sure that my great-great-great-great-grandfather, Zebediah 'the Conqueror' McManus, took a handball aboard the *Niña* as it set sail for a new West Indies spice route in

Handy fact! Michael 'Duxie' Walsh is the most successful handballer ever in terms of Irish championships. All-Ireland senior softball champ between 1985 and 1997, he was also a World finalist and won truckloads of other titles, none of which I bothered to note down for inclusion here. Sorry.

Handy fact!

None other than Tom Jones was Irish professional handball champion from 1888 to 1890, but he never played the game again because he became a priest. He later forged a successful career in cabaret entertainment.

1492, and even persuaded Columbus to play a few games against the wall of the below-deck torture chamber.

An Irish championship actually predated the foundation of the GAA, though the fledgling organisation formalised some rules at its third meeting in 1885. These included: courts of sixty-five feet; a ball weighing around two ounces; and players' bristling moustaches to measure at least seven inches from nostril to tip. Though subsequently rather disorganised in Mother Ireland, the game caught on like wildfire in the United States, even being promoted in their armed services (makes a nice distraction from bombing poor countries and squashing beer cans against your forehead, I suppose). The world championships were first held in 1964 in New York, with six

countries competing by 1984. The first televised matches were – *quelle surprise* – in the US in 1950, and rules were actually altered to allow fixed-time games for television during an RTÉ-broadcast tournament in 1980, hosted by the deep-voiced fella off *Bosco*, and with commentary by one or other of Aonghus McAnally's different coloured shoes.

Such a rich heritage, such incredible tales of derring-do, heroism and neon-haired castrato puppets … and still we, like the ungrateful little bastards we are, turned our backs on this noble art. But won't we look silly

Handy fact!

Irish emigrants took the game abroad and, in America, the young Abraham Lincoln was reputed to have played. A proposed face-off in a neutral ball-alley with Jefferson Davis, president of the seceded Confederate States of America, sadly never came to pass.

when the inevitable nuclear holocaust arrives, and the only structures left standing are those dependable old handball alleys? Hmm. I wonder will the cockroaches let us join them…

Handy fact!

Attempts to have handball included on the Olympic programme for Los Angeles in 1932 narrowly failed. Which is ludicrous, really, when you consider that such idiocies as mountain-biking, beach volleyball and Graeco-Roman wrestling have made the cut.

THE MAGIC ROUNDABOUT

We Europeans are always bemoaning how everything American eventually catches on over here, so it's nice to turn the tables the odd time. And you can't get a bigger table to turn than baseball, the iconic sport of 'God's own country'. On a social, cultural and historical level, baseball is king, and has become an integral part of the national myth.

Which makes it doubly amusing to know that the sport is descended from our game of rounders, a favoured pastime of balmy childhood summer evenings and one of the sports officially promoted by the GAA. Oh sure, Yanks will deny this, claiming that it was started by *Mayflower* pilgrims who used the leg of a slaughtered Indian to bat the head of a devoured turkey and then developed from there, or some such nonsense. We, of course – being European – know better. But we won't create a big fuss; let them have their 'baseball'. We'll just make do with the Renaissance, Shakespeare, the birth of democracy and Kraftwerk.

But how similar are our two games? I've put on my brainiest cap of all to find out.

	Baseball	**Rounders**
How to play:	Hit a ball with a stick	Hit a ball with a stick
And then?	Run around trying to catch it	Run around trying to catch it
Terminology:	Innings, slider, pitcher, Mendoza Line	I've to go home for my tea or my Mam will kill me

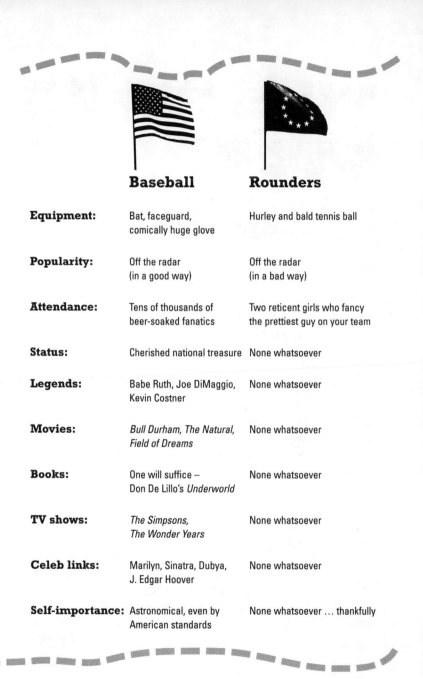

Baseball Rounders

	Baseball	**Rounders**
Equipment:	Bat, faceguard, comically huge glove	Hurley and bald tennis ball
Popularity:	Off the radar (in a good way)	Off the radar (in a bad way)
Attendance:	Tens of thousands of beer-soaked fanatics	Two reticent girls who fancy the prettiest guy on your team
Status:	Cherished national treasure	None whatsoever
Legends:	Babe Ruth, Joe DiMaggio, Kevin Costner	None whatsoever
Movies:	*Bull Durham*, *The Natural*, *Field of Dreams*	None whatsoever
Books:	One will suffice – Don De Lillo's *Underworld*	None whatsoever
TV shows:	*The Simpsons*, *The Wonder Years*	None whatsoever
Celeb links:	Marilyn, Sinatra, Dubya, J. Edgar Hoover	None whatsoever
Self-importance:	Astronomical, even by American standards	None whatsoever … thankfully

THIS RULES, DUDE!

Although its genesis dates back to the 1960s – when football teams toured Australia and **Aussie Rules** sides returned the compliment – and its modern revival is over twenty years old, the Compromise/International Rules series has never really taken off. This hybrid seems to have all the necessary attributes of a top-class field sport – exciting, tough, high-scoring and driven by a terrific kinetic energy – but lacks that X factor which separates the men from the lawn bowling. The public sort of has an interest, in Ireland at least, but I suspect this has more to do with people looking for something to do of an October Sunday, and wanting to keep that high summer vibe going for as long as possible, than any deep-felt love of the sport.

Anyway, all of this is now moot, since the series has been put on hold for 2007 by the GAA, after unacceptable levels of violence from the barbarous Antipodean hordes over the past few years. To be honest, the cynical part of me always believed that this was pretty much the main attraction for most people; that we tuned in because, not in spite, of the likelihood of bone-shattering, on-field ructions. Running battles which lasted for ten minutes, psychotic midget Aussie goalkeepers sprinting the length of the field to join in, torn shirts and dislocated noses … it was like Saturday night outside my local chipper with a ball thrown in, and it was compulsive viewing.

But in a more civilised world, such things are no longer acceptable. So how to spice up the flagging International Rules concept, if it's ever resuscitated in the first place? Just follow these imaginative, albeit a tad reckless, suggestions.

Swap the round ball for an oval one.

Not only would this make it fairer on the Australians, who are used to playing with a rugby-shaped ball, but unpredictable bounces and comical mishandling would enliven the sport as a spectacle.

Hurl insults at each other for three weeks beforehand.

The Aussies could slag us off about the Famine, Donie Cassidy and our litter problem, while we could retaliate with surgical strikes on *Home and Away*, maltreatment of the Aborigines and the fact that everyone in Australia is a sheep-shagging redneck with a terrible accent.

Choose a neutral venue.

Circumvent the problem of differing time zones by playing tests somewhere in the middle, like, say … oh, I dunno … Afghanistan or Iraq or somewhere. As a bonus, players would have to dodge incoming bombers and outgoing anti-aircraft fire, giving an added frisson of excitement.

Up the stakes considerably.

Start a war between Ireland and Australia over something stupid — pretty much how most wars start — and duke it out on the International Rules field. Kofi Annan can be roped in as referee, with George Mitchell and General de Chastelain as umpires, and the games can be fought/played in accordance with the Geneva Convention on Acceptable Conduct in Warfare and Makey-Uppy Games that Nobody Really Cares About.

If none of this works, I would like to propose my own compromise game that I'm sure the public will go wild for. I present to you: rugling. Played with a Wavin hurley and foam rugby ball, players score a 'troint' by hitting the ball over the bar, then running around the back and sliding through the grass with it. Or something. And in keeping with the theme of ultra-violence, tackling involves repeatedly punching the guy next to you in the scrum. Whether he's one of the opposition or not.

What about it, Central Council? I'm in the book if you get the urge to talk.

SHIN SHIN

Long before the bruisers from Down Under brought their rapid-fire fists and hilariously macho sleeveless shirts to the Compromise Rules arena, Gaels were engaging in international action. Unfortunately, that action happened to be in shinty-hurling, a recurring event with a profile so low that it is estimated only fourteen people have ever heard of it. Which is funny, because at least a hundred must have played in it.

At the risk of offending my many Scottish fans, shinty – or camanacht – is very much the poor man's hurling, with crowds for their version of the All-Ireland final barely squeaking past 5,000. Some scholars reckon, though, that it might have been played in Scotland for as long as hurling has been played in Ireland. The only explanation for its subsequent waning fortunes is that the Scots were too busy setting up banks, rolling their 'r' sounds and getting drunk on engine oil to be bothered promoting a trivial field sport. Or, if that doesn't work for you, here's the real reason: a wave of puritanism in the 1750s wiped out Sunday sport and, consequently, most traces of shinty, and it was proscribed by the British after a failed rising in 1745. Nowadays, the game is mainly restricted to the West and Central Highlands, which should help those endless freezing winters, endured with only a lonely mountain goat for company, go that bit quicker.

Anyway, despite its near-obliteration, we have been playing internationals against the shinty chaps since the 1924 Tailteann Games. Obviously, Ireland has generally been kicking ass and taking names – the fact that we have a big *bas* on the stick probably helps us control the ball a little better – but the Scots have sprung a few surprises. Though not as big a surprise as if they really did drink engine oil to pass the time.

FOREIGN GAMES
AND WHAT'S WRONG WITH THEM

As mentioned earlier, I hold no truck with all this 'sporting ecumenism' business. I used to, mind you – I played soccer in the schoolyard every evening, avidly followed the national soccer and rugby teams and athletes, and once won a fair wedge of money on the Aintree Grand National. But not no more, no sirree.

Why? Because I got burned too often by the bitter, vindictive and frankly incomprehensible anti-GAA agenda of a depressingly large section of this society. A case of many times bitten, twice shy, you might say. While not wishing any specific ill upon them, I do not desire success for the representative teams of competing sports. The GAA is strong enough to survive any number of soccer World Cups or hyped-up Lions tours, but that's irrelevant, and this is a point of principle. I want *our* games to thrive and couldn't give a fig about the strength of Irish 'football' or any other sport. And if you don't like that, then you should probably put the book aside at this point.

Anyway, it's nothing but a statement of fact that foreign games are, well, foreign. They originated in a different country, whether their adherents here want to acknowledge that or not. There's nothing rhetorically incorrect about the term. And besides, our native sports really are better. They're skilful, exciting, tough and honourable. And they make these sorry excuses for games wilt in comparison.

Foreign game: SOCCER
What's wrong with it: Dull, self-indulgent, played by the cretinous and followed by the spiteful.

Foreign game: BASKETBALL
What's wrong with it: Have to be an eleven-foot tall freak to properly compete.

Foreign game: RUGBY
What's wrong with it: Bull-necked jocks bashing heads and chewing ears for no good reason.

➡️ ·········

73

Foreign game: SQUASH
What's wrong with it: Too sweaty and noisy.

Foreign game: VOLLEYBALL
What's wrong with it: Only of interest to morose citizens of former Soviet satellites.

Foreign game: SNOOKER
What's wrong with it: No sport should involve the wearing of dickie-bows.

Foreign game: TENNIS
What's wrong with it: If they're not grunting on court, they're moaning about something or other off court.

Foreign game: CRICKET
What's wrong with it: Puffed-up old farts doddering around Albion's fair greens.

Foreign game: LAWN BOWLS
What's wrong with it: Puffed-up old farts still doddering around Albion's fair greens.

Foreign game: GOLF
What's wrong with it: The spiritual home of greedy conformists who are deeply afraid of women.

Foreign game: HACKY-SACK
What's wrong with it: Actually, I'll allow this one. Duuuude!

The competitions

The championship:
annual return of the king

Summertime – for many it signifies such delights as sunburn, melting ice-cream and a raft of rubbish programmes being rerun on television. Although those repeats of *The Prisoner* a few years back were pretty entertaining, to be fair. But, for others, the summer means something far more exciting. Yes, even more exciting than reruns of *The Prisoner*.

It means the championship is back. No more empty Sundays wondering why they don't just abolish the day and make it a double Saturday. No more daytime drinking and forcing yourself to watch that Tyrone Power melodrama yet again. No, those times are finished for ever (or until September at least). The king is back in the building.

Ah, the championship. Even the name is resonant and evocative, conjuring up images of sunny afternoons, fresh-cut grass, fat guys wearing T-shirts two sizes too small and swallowing a Dairy Milk all in one go. The memories are precious and infinite – parking four miles from the ground because traffic in town is like Jakarta during a riot; resisting the urge to point out that the urinals are actually there for a reason; grappling with ethical dilemmas: should I flirt with that fox in the Galway jersey or stay true to my county? (Always a tough one.)

The inter-county championship has certainly come a long way from its humble beginnings in 1887. So humble were they, in fact, that I'm not sure anyone at all even took part. Then, for the next three decades or so, the organisers couldn't seem to get the thing finished in the proper calendar year. So, for instance, we had the 1890 final played in 1892, that year's decider in 1903, and the 1903 final, oddly enough, run off some eight years previously. (Note: I am open to minor correction on these dates.)

But it has steadily evolved and matured and strengthened ever since then (if I was an *Irish Times* writer, I would at this point draw a parallel with the nation as a whole). In fact, the championship has now grown into such an enormous, omni-potent, all-devouring behemoth that some people are beginning to ask that most cautious of all questions: Is This A Good Thing? On the upside, it's driven the expansion in exposure and interest in the national games, with beneficial side-effects of increased participation and membership. On the downside, because most everything else gets put on hold for the champi-onship's duration, all those enthusiastic newbies often don't get a game between April and October.

Is it a good thing? Hell, I don't know. Some counties manage to run off their local competitions just fine throughout the summer, with little adverse effect on the county team's success. Others seem to enter a collective catatonic state round about the time Michael Lyster says, 'Hello, and welcome to the new series of *The Sunday Game*,' and don't snap out of it until crapped on the head by a passing bird on its way south for the winter.

All I know is that since the age of reason dawned for me, the championship has been the fulcrum around which my summers have revolved. Its hold may have waxed and waned over the years, its luminescence sometimes dimming from white-hot to a cooler red, but it's always, always been there, and always will. As an advert once put it, 'The GAA championship: heartbeat of the Irish summer.' Amen to that.

YOU'VE JUST GOTTA LOVE THAT

Five particular reasons for holding the championship in such affection.

LEAVING EARLY TO BEAT THE TRAFFIC

I have to laugh at how some folks, who have paid good money to be there, inevitably get itchy feet with five minutes remaining and decide not to bother watching the rest of the game. Sure, we'll get it on the radio.

IN A PERFECT WORLD: Supporters would be manacled to their seats/terrace stanchions by unbreakable futuristic energy beams.

IN A NIGHTMARE WORLD: The players would leave with five minutes left as well.

FINDING NEW WAYS OF BEATING THE TRAFFIC

Imitate Jack Kerouac in heading for parts unknown! Imitate rally ace Austin McHale as you navigate impassable dirt-tracks at high speed! Imitate that chubby guy off *Deliverance* when you lose your way and fall into the greasy hands of sex-crazed hillbillies with a disturbing fondness for pigs!

IN A PERFECT WORLD: You would own a KITT-style self-aware vehicle which whisks you home as you sleep, eat and laugh at Pete Finnerty's inaccurate predictions.

IN A NIGHTMARE WORLD: You'd get a puncture and discover you'd left the spare at home. During a rainstorm.

RUMOUR AND INNUENDO

People love to gossip and speculate, and inter-county provides us with ample material: injuries to key players, bust-ups with management, star forward spotted on the lash with certain well-known TV personality until eight in the morning, etc.

IN A PERFECT WORLD: Scurrilous (though untrue) rumours would unsettle the opposition just enough for your team to capitalise.

IN A NIGHTMARE WORLD: Scurrilous rumours about your own team would prove to be completely true.

THAT SICK FEELING IN THE PIT OF YOUR STOMACH JUST BEFORE THROW-IN

I could never figure out why anyone gets tanked up before a match, because it dulls the senses and thus deprives you of that beautifully keen edge of anxiety. You're *supposed* to face the prospect of defeat with something approaching mortal dread. Sure, it's horrible at the time, but makes winning all the sweeter.

IN A PERFECT WORLD: All those pent-up, broiling emotions would explode outwards in relief and joy as the final whistle signifies victory.

IN A NIGHTMARE WORLD: The guy behind you would puke on your shirt with nerves.

ANNOYING GAA-HATERS

Hey, I'm a magnanimous fellow. But there is something deliciously pleasurable about annoying those narrow-minded assholes who have an axe to grind with Gaelic games and the people who follow them. And it doesn't get any better than high summer: huge attendances, skyrocketing TV ratings, great atmosphere … in direct contrast to the miserable crowds and general air of decline which attend the League of Ireland.

IN A PERFECT WORLD: GAA-bashing types would be forced to sit through a two-hour compilation of the most mind-numbingly tedious post-match interviews.

IN A NIGHTMARE WORLD: More people would go to see the FAI Cup final than a bog-standard championship match. But that'll never happen, will it?

FIVE INDICATORS THAT YOUR TEAM IS GOING WELL

1 Huge signs proclaiming 'Good luck on Sunday lads' are planted in a ditch, obscuring the view at a dangerous bend.

2 Fertiliser bags of a colour vaguely resembling the county jersey are strung across the road.

3 Fertiliser bags of a colour not at all resembling the county jersey are strung across the road.

4 People with zero previous interest in GAA annoyingly ask everyone they meet, 'How will we do in the match?'

5 God – that *is* really annoying, isn't it?

GOOD LUCK LADS!

We can always hope
– SOME LONG DROUGHTS RECENTLY ENDED

DONEGAL: All-Ireland football 1992. **Waiting for:** ever

DERRY: All-Ireland football 1993. **Waiting for:** ditto

ARMAGH: All-Ireland football 2002. **Waiting for:** see above

TYRONE: All-Ireland football 2003. **Waiting for:** *ibid.*

WESTMEATH: Leinster football 2004. **Waiting for:** the same

ONLY the strong survive

Consider these few figures: Kerry have won more than a quarter of all senior football All-Irelands. Between them, Cork, Tipperary and Kilkenny have captured roughly two-thirds of all hurling championships. Nine counties have never won a senior All-Ireland in either code. Fermanagh and Wicklow are still waiting for their first senior *provincial* title.

On it goes. By its nature, there's more losing than winning in sport, and simple maths will work out that thirty-two counties into a handful of major prizes is a pretty tight squeeze. And by *our* nature, GAA folk are good-hearted and kind, and tend to take pity on those less fortunate members of our happy family. Like Longford and Monaghan and all them. ➡️
We apply delicate sobriquets like 'so-called weaker counties', when

CORK: All-Ireland football and hurling double 1990. **Waiting for:** 90 years

CLARE: All-Ireland hurling 1995. **Waiting for:** 81 years

CLARE: Munster football 1992. **Waiting for:** 74 years

LEITRIM: Connacht football 1994. **Waiting for:** 67 years

LAOIS: Leinster football 2003. **Waiting for:** 57 years

KILDARE: Leinster football 1998. **Waiting for:** 40 years

WATERFORD: Munster hurling 2002. **Waiting for:** 39 years

KERRY: All-Ireland football 2006. **Waiting for:** not very long, really

really there's no 'so-called' about it: they *are* weaker, and the record books are there to prove that this has been the case for twelve decades.

We suggest various tweaks to the competition structures in a bid to level the playing pitch between all counties, though I often wonder if some people's motivation isn't a more egalitarian system, but a cheap dig at the head honchos in Croke Park. Certain commentators are never happy, regardless of what is suggested. Hold on to the provincial system and all those poor souls are enchained by antiquated nonsense; introduce a second-chance saloon and you're making a mockery of the notion of knockout fare. The decision-makers just can't win, it seems. One genius, advocating the abolition of the Munster hurling championship, even blamed sentimentality for its retention. I'm sorry – what the hell other reason is there for following sport at all, when you come down to it? It's irrational and impractical by definition.

Anyway, about a decade ago, we finally moved away from the time-honoured structures, beginning with Nickey Brennan's far-sighted proposal for a back door in hurling. Since then, we've seen a qualifier system introduced for both games, the division of the hurling championship into three tiers and the inauguration of three new competitions: the Christy Ring and Nicky Rackard cups for hurling, and the Tommy Murphy Cup for football. And has it made much difference?

Mmm, sort of. The Big Three (or Two, really) now dominate hurling as much as ever, and will probably continue to do so, but football has seen the renascent rise of Ulster power and several encouraging breakthroughs, either in the provinces or qualifiers (Sligo, Fermanagh, Laois, Westmeath, Limerick, *et al*). But ultimately, all the modifications in the world are unlikely to make, say, Mayo into a hurling superpower. Only hard work, changing demographics and attitudes, coaching programmes and the benevolent blessings of a celestial deity can do that. And even then, in all probability, Mayo will never be a match for Kilkenny.

Call it Gaelic Darwinism if you like but, as in ecology, so in GAA: elephants squash gnats, polar bears eat Arctic explorers, Tyrone knock seven shades out of Carlow. Such is life, and there's not much Croke Park can do about it. ■

THE FINAL INSULT

'And now the end is near ... and two teams face the final curtain ...

My friends I'll say it clear ... who's gonna win? I'm far from certain ...

They've done what they had to do ... they've travelled

each and every highway (on the way to training) ...

But more, much more than this ...

They did it ... by being focused, committed,

having the hunger and being a great bunch of laahh–aaahhds...'

**Thanks for that, Frank. Direct from purgatory, folks,
Mr Frank Sinatra!**

Autumn – what a lovely time of year. Beautiful colours on the trees, cool wistful evenings, me laughing at sulky-faced teenagers who have to go back to school for another year … oh, and the All-Ireland finals. Whilst reflecting on this starlit marker in the Irish cultural firmament, I roughly worked out what percentage of them have been any good. And you'll be unpleasantly unsurprised, I think, to discover that poor quality is every bit as much a part of final day as the inevitable guy in a wheelchair tearing across the pitch on two wheels in post-match celebration.

Indeed, it's one of the great ironies of sport in general that the showpiece broadcast around the world to rapt millions, the archetypal 'advertisement for the game', often isn't particularly good. And All-Ireland finals can disappoint, too, though perhaps not as often because of a higher frequency of scores and the strong possibility of a minor riot in the tunnel at half-time. I've been watching since the early 1980s, and while the day itself never fails to be a colourful, exuberant occasion, a goodly proportion of the actual matches have been disappointing.

It all started, ominously enough, at the first final I attended, the hurling in 1982, when Kilkenny eviscerated their opponents Cork. The sense of anticlimax was alleviated, though, by the fact that I was only nine and didn't particularly care either way. At that age, you're more interested in peeling chewing gum off the concrete. Since then, really only 1986, 1990, 1993, 1997, 2001 and 2005 have cut the mustard, a pretty poor return for two-and-a-half decades. Surrounding these islands of quality has been a veritable Atlantic of dross, with the following so bad as to make part of my brain involuntarily shut down to avoid remembering them fully.

1985: Galway hand the title to Offaly by hitting approximately 115 wides (exact figures still unknown).

1989: A one-sided farce (see also 2000, 2002, 2004).

1995: Look beneath the romance, and Clare's victory over Offaly was achieved in a dreadful, laborious game.

1996: Likewise for Wexford.

1999: Cork and Kilkenny play out the lowest-scoring battle of attrition since the days of the forfeit point.

Oddly, there has been a slightly higher proportion of decent football finals in my lifetime, despite that code's reputation for soul-sucking destructiveness and paucity of entertainment. Offaly's legendary pickpocketing of Kerry in 1982 was, well, legendary. Other fine contests include 1989, 1991, 1992, 1998, 2000 (both days), 2002 and 2005. Obviously, though, the big ball game has foisted several stinkers upon us, too, with these little beauties among those automatically consigned to the section of long-term memory marked 'Catastrophes, disasters and other things best left untouched'.

1983: Dublin's Dirty Dozen somehow beats Galway's fourteen in windswept fiasco.

1987: Cork and Meath force us to sit through a turgid dogfight (see also 1988, 1990 and 1999).

1994: Notable only for the fact that Charlie Redmond missed yet another crucial penalty.

84

2001: Meath, for once, on the receiving end of a hammering.

2003: Tyrone and Armagh bring the concept of 'cagey' to new lows.

2006: Mayo freeze once more in a final against Kerry, to tragic, painful effect.

So there you have it, fact-fans – of the fifty-odd All-Ireland finals I have witnessed in my short and ultimately pointless existence, most have been rubbish, a few were okay, a smattering were pretty good and the odd, isolated freak was a classic. Encouraging and heart-warming statistics, I'm sure you'll agree. I would give you the percentage breakdown of good/bad ratios and graph curves, and so on, but that would just be too sad to even contemplate.

☑ **Bag of nerves**

☑ **Hurricane George**

☑ **A world of hype**

Five guarantees for a rubbish All-Ireland final

1. The match is broadcast in every country in the world, hundreds of dignitaries are in attendance and the year is an anniversary of some important GAA event.
2. One of the teams is final virgins and, consequently, suffers a crippling attack of stage fright. Alternatively…
3. Both teams know the other inside out, preferably with an unfinished grudge hanging about from the previous year.
4. A strong breeze blowing down the pitch (if not available, a swirly one will do) accompanied by biblical rainfall for three days beforehand.
5. And the kiss of death: the match is widely described as 'a potential classic'. The greater the expectation, the greater the let-down. This is a scientific fact.

Tickets, please!

The attendances at All-Ireland finals often contain fewer fans of participating counties than the semi-finals. If this seems weird to you, don't worry, because it's weird to me too.

Every year, this gnarly subject finds itself at the forefront of public affairs. It's debated at the UN, protested about on urban battlegrounds, discussed by pretentious tossers on late-night arts programmes. Families have been cleaved apart, fortunes squandered and reputations ruined in a vain attempt to secure access to the day of all days.

You see, All-Ireland tickets are divvied up between the whole country. This is because the final is seen as a Great Social Event and National Occasion, as well as a sporting contest. The president greets the teams, some bull-throated tenor gets wheeled out for the anthem, the match is broadcast internationally for mournful ex-pats in bars across the world. It's part of our cultural heritage, like Paddy's Day or the hung-over day after Paddy's Day. Thus, everyone should have the chance to experience this great moment in Irish life.

Now, I can sort of see the point in allowing a few tickets for counties like Monaghan and Carlow, who will probably never reach that level them-selves (not in this dimension anyway). It's a pleasant trip to Croker, a taste of the atmosphere and colour. But not half of them, for God's sake. That's madness. Like, basic logic will figure out that if you give all the tickets away, there are none left for the counties involved, and the atmosphere for which neutrals are paying won't be there in the first place. It can't be much fun sitting in an enormous amphitheatre filled with 80,000 people chatting politely about what a grand day it is, eating ice-cream and asking when the bull-throated tenor is on.

Why can't there be some balance in ticket distribution? Fine, give a few thousand to weaker counties. Spread it around a little – I'm a generous guy.

But not three or four to every club in every weaker county. Let 'em find their own All-Ireland to go to. Then maybe we wouldn't have to resort to extreme (and sometimes illegal) lengths to get our grubby little hands on some of that cardboard gold. If I had a dollar for every time some desperate soul has phoned me in the middle of the night, pleading for tickets, I'd be off down to the *bureau de change* to get $6.50 converted into euro. The breadth and creativity of bribes I've been offered is mind-boggling: cash, classified substances, sexual favours of a distinctly non-canonical nature, at least fourteen stellar constellations named after me, a secret map which provides directions to a buried chest of pirate treasure, the works.

Indeed, I was often that soldier myself, trawling the underworld for a hint, a sniff, a rumour of a ticket. One year, there were about ten of us itching to go to the final and, of course, fewer than ten tickets to go around. My dad had to show commendable ingenuity in procuring admission for us, including (but not limited to) relatives up the country, well-connected friends and torture. I don't really want to go into too many details, but suffice it to say a darkened bunker, two electrodes and a hungry Alsatian were involved. Thanks, pops – we'll always be grateful.

Until next year, anyway.

Diary of a fan on final day

The glory, the passion, the eight hours stuck in traffic – All-Ireland final day encapsulates all this and more. Here, we present exclusive extracts from *I'm Just Waiting for the Celtic Tenors – Diary of a Fan on Final Day*. (Note: the author will be reading from a selection of his work in the upstairs toilet of the Red Cow on All-Ireland final eve. Please book early to avoid disappointment.)

08.00: Alarm goes off. Fail to hear it because of drink-induced partial coma. Went on massive bender after mass last night to get into mood for today. McCafferty arrested for lewd behaviour and Bingo died when heart imploded — craic was mighty.

08.40: Awoken from coma by dog chewing on foot. Make huge fry to steady nerves. Dog eats huge fry to steady his nerves. Substitute with pot of tea and twenty Major.

09.11: Realise train leaving in four minutes. Jam Cordoba over to station.

10.05: Train late leaving, which was good. Two-thirds of entire county already on it, which was bad. Decide to drive.

12.40: Engine explodes at Portlaoise. Half-assed attempt to fix it by plugging holes with Moxer's replica jersey. Who'd have thought synthetic material is so flammable? Decide to hitch.

13.20: Still no sign of a lift. What is so unappealing to drivers about four grown men in Viking horns carrying trays of Guinness?

13.40: Half the porter drunk, egg sangwiches gone toxic and missing minor match. Try to tune into radio commentary via Paudie's gold fillings. No luck, although do pick up interesting documentary on leather production in former Eastern Bloc countries.

14.08: Finally wangle lift with guts lorry heading for the ferry. Promptly pass out from the smell.

15.11: Croker at last! Looming before us like, um . . . a big looming concrete thing. Stride purposefully to turnstile before realising ticket is gone from pocket. Blasted truck driver — thought he was just being affectionate.

➡️

15.13: So-called friends have deserted both me and forty-eight empty Guinness cans. Spot tout with sparse moustache bellowing, 'Aneeewon buyinorsellin' detiggedsdere?' Must be some kind of insider lingo. Mooch on over to 'make the deal'.

'How much for a stand ticket?'

'Tree hundred, bud.'

'No way I'm paying three hundred to watch a match.'

'Your loss. 'Course, I could always bribe someone to let you in for a tenner. Get you a grand aerial view hangin' on to de scoreboard ... dough possibly lengtening de odds on your survival slightly.'

'Why, you dirty, dishonest motherfuc— ... ah yeah, go on, so.'

15.32: Ball is in and game is on! And I'm hanging on for dear life from pole several hundred feet high! Manage to fasten leg securely with woolly scarf and settle down to watch game.

15.47: Dirty looks from TV crews. Claim my fevered swearing being picked up by boom mike and heard across world. What do they expect? That was never a penalty.

16.08: Half-time, and still in it. TV crew has threatened to have guards eject me if I don't stop shouting abuse at opposition. Say they've received two hundred calls of complaint. I'm a star! If the lads could only see me now! ➡

16.40: Struggle with two gardaí and coterie of maors broadcast on huge screen on the Hill. Crowd becomes more interested in this than in match for about three minutes. Then fight starts in goalmouth and they lose interest.

17.00: Game arrives at thrilling climax. Gardaí, maors and I momentarily turn attention to action on the pitch, forgetting differences for a little while. Ah, the healing power of sport.

17.03: Combination of winning goal, full-time whistle, scarf unravelling and obscene weight of one maor sends whole shooting gallery down on top of commentary box. Ger Canning becomes latest person heard swearing on prime-time TV, cameraman buried alive under obese maor, and I crash through floor into Uachtarán's lap.

17.04: Try to think of something polite to say. 'Sorry I dented the cup so badly. I know a panel-beater who'll do a job on it on the cheap for you, though.' He's lost for words; carried away by occasion, I guess.

17.09: Final, fond farewell to crowds, Uachtarán and assorted members of the guards as I'm led away into high-security prison van. Smile with affection on day's events. Stop smiling when I realise I could be facing a hefty jail sentence.

→

18.15: (written in cell 4D, tier 3, block AJ: Ah, God bless All-Ireland final day — the glory, majesty, exuberant colour . . . and not forgetting the fact that everyone is welcome, even a complete gobsheen like me.

I'm Just Waiting for the Celtic Tenors: Diary of a Fan on Final Day is published by Blackguard Press, priced at €65 hardback (some copies may be missing a cover) and from €1.50 paperback, working swiftly downwards.

GET WITH THE PROGRAMME

'Programme! Programme! Gedyoorohfeeshall programme!'

'Programme! Programme! Gedyoorohfeeshall programme!'

The instantly recognisable – and incredibly irritating – cry of the big-match programme-seller, usually a ruddy kid with a bag slung over his shoulder and a maximum volume utterly disproportionate to his minuscule frame. If you close your eyes and concentrate really hard, you can pretend momentarily that these are actually young street urchins of Victorian London, hawking that day's newspaper which covers the latest Whitechapel murder in grisly detail. Unlike with nineteenth-century street urchins, though, you're not allowed to then hit them a clout and bellow contemptuously, 'Out of my way, you rabble! Upstanding servant of the crown coming through!'

'Programme! Programme! Gedyoorohfeeshall programme!'

Which is a pity, because match programmes really, really suck, don't they? And you have to take the disappointment out on somebody. Programmes have sucked for as long as I can remember, beginning with the 1985 provincial semi-final at which I got gipped for fifty pence by some crook selling photocopied imitations. You can imagine my shock when, on eagerly opening the document to the centre pages, I beheld the wrong teams printed in the wrong order in a horrendous green ink. And the rest of it was so rubbish that the dog later refused to sleep on it, claiming to have 'some standards'.

Still, I shouldn't have taken it too badly, as the official version is never much better. For your three euro – or is it now four? – what do you get, exactly? Glossy paper: big deal. Team lists: wow, I'm impressed. Some piffling statistics: good God, my heart can't take the excitement. The rest of the average programme is padded out with lots of advertising, a few hokey player profiles, numerous factual errors, a poorly written 'remember when?' piece, and an address from some official or other which is so dreary that it makes *The Gulag Archipelago* read like the backstage diaries of Axl Rose in his pomp. And to add insult to daylight robbery, the page size has increased to the point where it no longer folds up and fits neatly into the pocket of your good match-day sports jacket.

'Programme! Programme! Gedyoorohfeeshall programme!'

I no longer bother purchasing these wretched rags, preferring to discreetly lean in and read the teams off the programme of the guy in front but, for many others, the habit is a hard one to break. Could I suggest that some scientific *wunderkind* develops a modified version of the nicotine patch, that we may wean chronic devotees off their addiction? Platitudes, flim-flam, incorrectly captioned photographs and a lingering sense that you've been screwed could be absorbed directly into the bloodstream through patches applied to the skin. And if that doesn't work, you can always take up smoking to ease the pain.

I WANT MY LEAGUE-A!

Zero temperatures, sub-zero crowds (hey, it's possible) and the sounding of the death knell … if recent coverage of the national league has one cohesive motif, it's the unrelentingly glum prophecies of doom and impending demise. The league, apparently, is a rickety cripple limping along with little purpose and less relevance, an embarrassing old relic, a waste of effort for people with more important matters on their minds.

But despite widespread derision the secondary competition, in my far-from-humble opinion, is still worth checking out. Sure, you may not have the huge TV audience, the indescribable rush of being surrounded by 50,000 passionate followers, the summer sun and hard green pitches. You mightn't even have a dry seat on which to park your weary butt. But true GAA fans still love going to league matches. For one thing, it's more enjoyable than championship in a way, because there is far less pressure. You can sit back and watch the game, comfortable that defeat isn't the end of the world.

Also, it's cool to see young, up-and-coming talent … um … up-and-come, I guess. There's a certain complicity in spotting who has what it takes, seeing the team take shape through the rain-soaked visors of early spring. (Plus you can act all superior when some young tyro does come through to star in June. 'Yeah, well *I* saw him score a goal even better than that in March … admittedly, their goalkeeper was stuck in mud up to his knees at the time.') And, of course, managing to reach a toilet and get served at the stadium shop are a lot simpler when you're not being buffeted around like the ping in a game of ping-pong.

But there's a more important reason for respect: barring half-assed affairs like the McKenna Cup, there are only two senior inter-county competitions in GAA, and the league is one. For many players, a league medal is the only bauble of any importance they will ever win. Why, then, this universal hostility?

Commentators point to the poor fare and dwindling attendances, but that's only part of the story. Yes, the standard can be pretty 'sub-' at times, but, dammit, that's what following sport is all about – suffering the slings and arrows of outrageous crud in the hope of a moment of beauty. And, yes, recent turnout for finals has generally been pathetic, but I'm a strong believer in the notion of self-fulfilling prophecies. Tell people enough times that something isn't worth bothering with and, well, they won't bother with it. Constant reference to how pointless the league is lodges in people's minds and convinces them to stay away, which, of course, leads to lower crowds, which leads to proclamations of the league's demise which leads to …
and so on *ad infinitum.*

So maybe the poor forlorn old league ain't so bad after all. Get aboard for the big push, soldier – show us whose side you're on. Quit yer moaning and get down to the nearest match. This is where the summer starts. (PS: Bring a flask of coffee – it's bloody *freezing* outside.) 🂠

for later

WE'LL 'FILE IT AWAY FOR LATER

The high/low point of any programme is the player profile, in which random team members give grudging answers to pointless questions. Should you ever find yourself in this awkward position, just use this helpful cut-out-and-keep guide, which covers all potentialities.

Name: (We can't help you with this one, unfortunately.)

Club: (Ditto.)

Age: (You know the drill by now.)

Biggest influence growing up: My father/my first teacher/Satan.

Favourite position: Anywhere in the first fifteen/wherever the head man wants me to go/the reverse Praying Lotus.

Rule you'd like to see changed: The tackle/the pickup off the ground/that of our Illuminati overlords.

Greatest thrill: Winning my first underage title/being selected for the seniors/absinthe, peyote and MDMA cocktail straight to the cerebral cortex.

▶

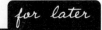

Greatest disappointment:
Losing the county final last
year/getting dropped by the
seniors/waking up the next
morning to discover I wasn't
actually the reincarnation of
Krishna.

Favourite star of yore:
Mick O'Connell/Seanie
O'Leary/Gloria Swanson.

Favourite food: Steak and
chips/fish and chips/tofu
fritters (and chips).

Favourite drink:
Coke/stout/the blood of a
freshly sacrificed virgin.

Favourite TV show: *The
Sunday Game/The Sopranos/
Mr Belvedere* reruns.

Favourite actor & actress:
Tom Hanks & Kate Winslett/
Tom Cruise & Cate Blanchett/
Divine (for both).

Favourite place: Connemara/
Malta/Tijuana docks.

Favourite item of clothing:
Levi's jeans/CK shirt/spiked
dog-collar with matching
chain-lead accessory.

Ambition: To win the All-Ireland/
to win the county/to win the
heart of that celebrity I've been
stalking since last November.

Everyone's a winner, baby
(NO, THAT'S A LIE)

It has almost become a scientific truth in the GAA consciousness (taking its place beside 'a sending-off is of more benefit to the fourteen-man team') that success in the league practically guarantees an early bath at championship level. The league, they say (well, mainly Micko) is a poisoned chalice, holding within certain disaster, as well as saliva-filled fizzy orange. But is this a valid presumption? Does winning the league put the kibosh on a team's chances of staying around past the June Bank Holiday? I have decided to put the theory to the test.

A team of top boffins at the Kashmir Institute of Higher Level Investigation into Spurious Statistical Link-Ups has spent the past ten minutes attempting to reach some sort of unifying conclusion. They fed every league winner of the past five years into the SPORTRON 5000© computer, entered their championship form and hit 'Analyse Jinx Measurement'. Here's what the printout had to say.

Hurling league champs

2002: Kilkenny. All-Ireland champions. Jinx rating: non-existent.
2003: Kilkenny. All-Ireland champions (again). Jinx rating: hmm. I'm beginning to doubt this theory very much.
2004: Galway. Absolutely freakin' annihilated in the qualifiers. Jinx rating: ah, that's better.
2005: Kilkenny. Narrowly lost All-Ireland semi-final. Jinx rating: medium.
2006: Kilkenny. All-Ireland champions. Jinx rating: yes, there is much doubt about the theory.

Football league champs

2002: Tyrone. Turfed out in shock defeat to Sligo. Jinx rating: high.
2003: Tyrone. All-Ireland champions. Jinx rating: non-existent.
2004: Kerry. Also All-Ireland champions. Jinx rating: am I detecting a pattern here?
2005: Armagh. Ulster champs but lost All-Ireland semi to hated rivals. Jinx rating: no, there's no pattern.
2006: Kerry. All-Ireland champions. Jinx rating: ooh, scratch that, there is a pattern. Well, there is when Mayo are your final opponents, anyhow.

LEAGUE ME Out OF this

It's confused us; it's misused us; it's run around town and abused us. But in between, the league has provided some moments of great interest. Prepare to be the envy of your friends and amaze complete strangers.

▲ The leagues were established in 1925 and immediately seen as A THREAT to the existing power-base, the club championships. Pretty ironic considering, huh?

▲ They were SUSPENDED in 1942 (some minor scuffle had broken out throughout 60 per cent of the globe). However, the suspension was successfully appealed on video evidence.

▲ The leagues in both codes have endured more reshuffles and structural changes than a MEXICAN GOVERNMENT. Football has had, among others, first and second north and south divisions, six divisions comprised of north 1, south 1, north 2A, south 2A, and so on, and regional divisions where the McKenna Cup winners represented Ulster.

▲ In hurling, a three-group experiment ran from 1929 to 1934, and round-robin competitions were run from 1934 to 1937, although proposals to form four 'Groups of Death', involving a bizarre hybrid of hurling, tae-kwon-do and SLASH-HOOK WIELDING, were defeated at congress. By one vote.

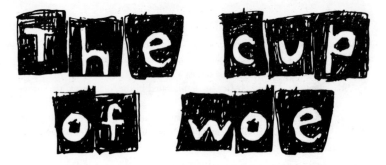

The cup of woe

Outside of the staples – championship, league and such-and-such – the GAA has a long history of unusual and downright peculiar competitions. Most of them are now long gone, but so are Elvis, feudalism and Cherry Coke, and we all still remember those fondly, don't we?

Centenary Cup (1984): Held in Centenary Year – like, obviously – this commemorated the centenary of the GAA, hence the apt title. Hmm … I could have phrased that more clearly. The following year saw the short-lived Open Draw competition – a sort of Son of the Centenary Cup.

Croke Cup (1896–1916): It went through a bewildering number of format changes, but believe it or not, the Croke Cup was once regarded as the GAA's second most important competition. Succeeded by the Wolfe Tone Tournament (I'm guessing in honour of the bewhiskered Republican balladeers).

Grounds Tournament (1961–1973): Pairing the beaten All-Ireland football semi-finalists against the winners of the other semi, this competition drew impressive crowds which, through some anti-logic of history, ensured its swift demise. Go figure.

Corn Oireachtais (1939 to present): After a tortuous route involving approximately 803 other competitions, the Oireachtas was eventually instigated to establish closer connections between the GAA and Gaelic League. (Early bonds had been forged by the barmy Captain Otway Cuffe, who wanted to revive knee breeches and woollen stockings as suitable dress for Irish boys. I kid you not.) A handful of people saw Limerick beat Kilkenny in the first final in November 1939; everyone else was watching the Battle of Warsaw on telly. The competition grew rapidly in popularity after 1946, then slowly reverted into unpopularity (if there is such a word). Nobody quite knows whether it still actually exists or not.

Railway Cup (1926 to present): Inter-provincial action

goes back to well before the GAA's foundation, with newspapers advertising matches in the eighteenth century. Presumably along the lines of: 'Hear ye, hear ye, subjects of the crown! The Right Honourable Sir Smedley Gordimer is proud to present, in association with Dr Treblecock's Molasses-Flavoured Vitalogy Elixir, the forthcoming footballing engagements. Admission: one Spanish doubloon. Special match-day hansom carriages running hourly from Mad Meg's Tavern.' The Railway Shield ran from 1910 to 1925, and the Railway Cup was inaugurated the following year. Attendances grew exponentially, averaging over 40,000 throughout the 1950s, the tournament's golden era. By the 1970s, alas, the competition was in serious decline, though it has managed to somehow dribble along since, despite seemingly universal apathy from spectators.

St Brendan's Cup (1954–1960): Played between the

league champs and New York, and won twice by the Yanks. Woo-yah! USA! USA! USA! etc., etc.

Wembley Tournament (1958–1976): The spiritual

home of English soccer became the temporary home of London GAA. Gor blimey, luv a duck, and so on.

World Cup (1967–1969): The rather self-importantly titled

World Cup was played between New York and the All-Ireland champs. One victory for New York in 1969. Woo-yah! USA! USA! USA! etc., etc. (again).

CLUBBed to deAth

It's winter, it's freezing/depressing in equally crushing measures, and the only reason to keep living is the prospect of a clean headshot on any member of Westlife at a music-awards ceremony. But soft! What light through yonder window breaks? 'Tis the concluding stages of the All-Ireland club championship (and 'tis actually breaking through the window – use the door, for God's sake!).

Since 1971, this has steadily established itself as one of GAA's foremost competitions, proving the age-old tenet that the club is the cornerstone of the association, and if you rock the foundations, then … um … the cradle will fall. I think. Anyway, whether you're doing it for the honour of the little village, or just to stick it to the neighbours whose county haven't won squat for twenty years, capturing this crown is the highest honour to which the average, non-Nobel Laureate clubman can aspire. So here's a club sandwich of tasty facts and figures.

1. Cork have won the most club titles, with a massive twenty between both codes. Gee, maybe it's true what my Corkie pals used to goad me with in college – you really *will* never beat the Rebels.

2. Nemo Rangers are the most honoured club, with a whopping seven crowns in football. Gee, maybe it's true what my Corkie pals, etc., etc. And not that far across the city, St Finbarr's are the only double winners, capturing two in hurling and three in football. Gee, maybe it's true, la, la, la, la, la.

3. Birr created history in 2003 by becoming the first club to win four hurling titles. Good for them.

4. Rathnure are the greatest losers in hurling, biting the big one in no fewer than five finals. Unusual, that, for a Wexford team. In football, the kings of pain are Roscommon's Clann na nGael, with a five for zero record in their final appearances, including a suicide-inducing four-in-a-row from 1987 to 1990. Ooh – that's gotta hurt.

5. The colleges have also got in on the glory act, with UCD putting back-to-back titles together in the 1970s, followed by Thomond a few years later. 'Cause students have rights, too, you know. Poor old UCC lost their one final in 1972, prompting a protest sit-in in the cafeteria and disruption of two weeks' sociology lectures.

What's another year?

One of the most bizarre GAA habits is playing county finals the year after the competition began. Junior and U21 are normally the most affected by fixtures pile-ups, inter-county success, inclement weather and protracted investigations into what really *did* cause the ref's car to explode after the semi-final. The problem can reach epidemic proportions; indeed, in remote parts of the West of Ireland, finals have been known to take place up to thirty years late. Naturally, this can cause severe confusion, with no one quite sure who is still eligible or not.

The fact that these matches are played in darkest January doesn't help. It's colder than Siberia, the players are still hung-over from Christmas, and the ground looks like a bunch of over-keen history students decided to re-enact the Battle of the Somme on it that morning. The size of the crowd (two proud mothers, four diehards currently awaiting their divorce papers and a homeless dog), invariably low scores and thick, ectoplasmic fog settling onto the pitch add to the surreal and deathly air.

But there's no excuse for this kind of carry-on. I mean, I can understand it happening back in the bad old days, when a veritable cornucopia of hindrances and obstacles presented itself. Let's face it, a game of football can seem a little off-putting when you've just coughed up half your stomach because of TB. Not to mention the Black and Tans shooting your full-forward line, the captain's arrest for sedition against the crown, the whole team emigrating to 'Americay', de Valera banning the game because one of the umpires was overheard remarking, 'You know, those cricket lads – they're not all bad', entire counties being quarantined because of an outbreak of bubonic plague, and so on.

Surely now, though, in this era of economic boom, aerodynamic transport and incredibly strong drugs to cure bubonic plague, we could manage to play this year's Leitrim Junior 'A' hurling league final … oh my God! … this year! But, apparently not.

Studying the form

The relationship between the GAA and this country's third-level institutions is a long and complex one. Well, it would have to be complex, wouldn't it? Bloody melodramatic students, always making a big deal out of everything. And, of course, they have to insist on their own competitions. What, you couldn't compete with the rest of us plebs? The small talk at the training ground isn't intellectually stimulating enough?

Trinity College, believe it or else, played a major role in fostering GAA in the nineteenth century (which is kinda ironic, considering that it could hardly get more West Brit if they painted a mural of Charles and Camilla on the entrance flagstones). The game of hurling was revived in part by Trinners students, who founded the Irish Hurley Union in 1879, resolving to 'foster the noble and manly art of hurley in its native country'. Admirable sentiments, but unfortunately not realised, as the group morphed into the Irish Hockey Union about a decade later. Stupidly enough.

Inter-varsity contests began in 1911 when UCD invited UCG and UCC to partake in competition. Once everyone managed to work out what exactly all those acronyms stood for, the Sigerson Cup was born. The hurling equivalent, the Fitzgibbon, was established the following year in UCC – a fine educational establishment, I must add, producing many talented and highly attractive people – and Cork won both inaugural titles. In your face, other third-level institutions!

After a while they let in RTCs, Ulster polytechnics and all kind of other tuppenny-ha'penny joints. Although Tralee IT, Waterford IT and UL have enjoyed success in recent years, the NUI colleges dominate the honours rolls. I'm fairly sure, anyway, that UCC won the Fitzgibbon pretty much every year I was there, although my memory of that time is a little hazy.

Many famous names have plied their sporting wares at college level. Dublin great Dr Pat O'Neill represented UCD. Much-loved **Sunday Game** star Pat Spillane won an All-Ireland club championship with Thomond College in 1978. And fellow Kingdom All-Ireland winner Colm Kennelly was one of the founders of Trinity GAA club, and later played rugby for British Guiana for some reason. Oh yeah, and his brother is the poet Brendan. SDLP politician Joe Hendron, Mary McAleese's husband Martin and chirpy television entertainer Patrick Kielty have all represented their college at some stage too.

A mysterious entity known as the Combined Universities entered the Railway Cup on an experimental basis in 1972, and although the footballers won one title, the experiment was not renewed. This decision could have led to mass unrest and civil disobedience by protesting students, were it not for the fact that nobody gave a rat's ass about the Railway Cup, even back then. But one victory the Combined Universities couldn't deliver was in a Compromise Rules fixtures against the Victorian Galahs in 1968. (I'm not making this up – that really was their name.) The stupidly named Antipodeans defeated our boys and reportedly celebrated by taunting their vanquished foes, 'Now who feels like a right Galah, huh? Answer me that, cobber!'

Gaelic games have become more globally dispersed over the past decade, what with cheap flights and mobile phones and the worldwide inter-web and that. But did you know that students in Tampere University in Finland began playing handball way back in the 1980s? Or that Chinese man Zhao Yinong became the first Finnish singles champion in 1990, and subsequently introduced the game to Beijing?

What, exactly, a Chinese person was doing playing an Irish sport in Finland is beyond me, but that's students for you – they're always up to some sort of crazy antics.

Um, training tips for student players, okay?

- Build upper-body strength with some window-smashing and Molotov cocktail-throwing at the next anti-globalisation riot.

- Take care of all nutritional needs with the good, wholesome fare of campus catering. But check to make sure nobody's put out their cigarette in your bowl of hog-fat soup.

- Improve concentration and mental discipline by cramming for twenty-six hours straight while subsisting on nothing but caffeine pills, battered sausages and ink sucked from your leaking biro.

- Work on your speed by racing fellow students to the bank to cash the weekly cheque from your parents.

- Discommode your direct opponent by declaring that all sport is meaningless because life itself is meaningless, then dig him in the ribs when he's not looking.

COOL ÁLAINN
(how GAA got trendy)

When I was a teenager, I was in a grunge band with my brother and our friend. Of course, being pedantic, we weren't a *real* group, if by 'real' you mean playing instruments, making records, and so on. But, anyway, we had this great idea for an album cover: a hurler hailing the crowd after scoring.

We thought this a real *zeitgeist*-forming masterstroke, a concept both original and audacious. Here was a sport so un-hip, so mocked by style gurus, so out of time that its alternative cachet was impeccable. Hurling was for thick culchies, mountain men belting each other with sticks in front of slack-jawed in-breds. Hurlers didn't model for Versace or date celebrities; they had rural accents and unfashionable haircuts. It was inconceivable

• •

Timeline –
the birth of (sponsored GAA) man

Prehistory

Late Paleantezoicassic

that one could like GAA *and* be into Soundgarden and philosophy and Elmore Leonard. Boringly cynical columnists wrote mocking, condescending pieces on 'bogball' and 'stickfighting'.

It was perfect. Our band would lay down a marker by naming the album *4.40pm Semple* or something, with the cover shot of Nicky English wheeling away after kicking the sliotar past Ger Cunningham in 1987. We were cool enough not to conform to others' expectations; we marched to our own off-kilter drum; we were unique.

HIP

And then whaddya know? Sometime in the early to mid-1990s, GAA went and got itself trendy. Hurling and football are officially now hip. They're even – I'm finding it difficult to form the word – sexy. No longer are matches the sole preserve of kids with their dads, ➡

The Middle Epoch   **Post-Reformation**   **The Future**

bunches of lads out for a skinful, and obsessive, socially unskilled nerds who've missed one game in the past twenty years, and only then because the house collapsed on them. No, cool young guys and dolls now toddle along to Páirc Uí Chaoimh or Croker for big matches. County jerseys are a common sight on campus. Rickety old stanchions on storm-tossed hillsides have been replaced by swish corporate boxes in a futuristic stadium. And almost everyone has some opinion on Galway's chances, the pay-for-play issue, and why, oh why, do Carlow wear those blindness-inducing dayglo jerseys?

SEXY

But how did this brave new world of coolness come to pass? Some would say it was representative of our maturing as a nation, a new-found ability to embrace our own culture. Me, I think Clare were responsible for a lot. When the Banner won the All-Ireland in 1995, they ignited a flame waiting to be lit. Their victory was so romantic, implausible and dramatic that it captured the imagination of the whole country. The following year, Wexford followed suit. It helped that both had colourful individuals in their team and management, but the important thing was that they were new, fresh and even, dare I say it, glamorous. The media coverage expanded in direct proportion to crowd sizes, as more and more returned, or came for the first time, to Gaelic playing fields.

Football had its share of attention-grabbers during that period, too, like the Meath–Dublin epic of 1991, Ulster's breakthrough and Kildare's resurrection (a county which defines modern-day GAA in many ways). And Guinness' sponsorship of the hurling championship, coincidentally also beginning in 1995, gave this evolution an extra little push. In keeping with the renowned quality of their advertising, the beer giants coined some memorable slogans and gave the championship a sleek, cinematic sheen. (The

COOL

recent 'He's an old man, Seanie. There's nothing I can do' advert is like a really cool hybrid of *The Sopranos*, *The Brothers McMullen* and a Denis Leary routine.) And, of course, the Bank of Ireland and other main sponsors subsequently upped their game, while more and more players struck individual sponsorship deals that didn't necessarily revolve around the most effective way of combating scour in calves.

Naturally, some things haven't changed. The toilets still usually stink, the same hawkers sell the same cans and chocolate from the same stalls, and those godawful straw cowboy hats will always be among us. (Which, you know, ain't necessarily so bad – it's nice to see a few old traditions hanging around. Nothing is worse than the sanitised luxury of, say, Champions' League soccer.) And these things can be overstated. Huge crowds have always attended, it's always been a pivotal part of our lives, and most importantly, I've gone to games all my life and I was always extremely cool. Though not as cool as our bass player, to be honest.

But, on balance, the image of GAA has changed utterly, with All-Ireland tickets replacing an annulled marriage and adopted Cambodian child as *the* designer accessory of the age. As for the future, will some iconic figure sound the death knell for our games by wearing a 'GAA is Dead' T-shirt, as Kurt Cobain once did for grunge? Will it collapse under the weight of its own success? Maybe. But for now, Gaelic games stand tall, a cultural phenomenon, the new rock 'n' roll.

Although now that I think about it, that's probably just until actual rock 'n' roll becomes the new rock 'n' roll again. So enjoy it while it lasts.

Die hard!

With many people now pretending to like Gaelic games because they think it's cool (which it is) and it'll help them make new friends (which it won't) and meet interesting people (depends on your definition of interesting), it's become increasingly difficult to tell the wheat from the chaff. In a manner of speaking. Who are the true-blue, old skool GAA heads, those doughty soldiers who stood on draughty terraces freezing their tender parts off for the meagre reward of spotting some future county talent? And, conversely, how can we tell the kind of people who now include GAA alongside MP3 technology and teaching TEFL in Barcelona in a list of their 'interests' … and thus eliminate them?

Here's how – fill in the patented Supportex 3000 Questionnaire below, tot up your score and discover exactly which kind of GAA fan you are. Then act accordingly, using the helpful step-by-step guide to self-annihilation. **Good luck!**

1. **What is your earliest memory of GAA?**
    a. Wondering vaguely what the point was after suffering a bloody nose whilst playing in an U7 tournament.
    b. Wondering vaguely what the point was as Fr Consumption, the U12 trainer, forced you to run backwards up the school hill with a bag of cement on your back.
    c. The opening of the new Hogan Stand.

2. **How do you celebrate an important victory?**
    a. Four days of drinking and absenteeism with constant verbal abuse towards opposition fans and some resolutely heterosexual bonding with your 'mates'.
    b. Four days of drinking and absenteeism accompanied by a good, healthy dose of guilt.
    c. Four days of drinking and absenteeism spent talking loudly in pretentious bars about the game while getting all the players' names wrong.

3. **What is your definition of the ideal match?**
    a. Beating the crap out of the team you lost to last year, ideally with their most loathsome player sent off as the icing on the cake.
    b. A whopping thirty-point victory achieved with style, character and panache – and their most loathsome player sent off as the icing on the cake.
    c. An exciting game played in the right spirit, with the underdog coming out on top in the end.

4. **Which of these are the most crucial things to bring to a big game?**
   a. Straw cowboy hat, tray of Smithwick's, large store of 'terrace wit'.
   b. Old newspaper to sit on, red lemonade and chicken legs, biro to note down each scorer on the programme.
   c. Mobile phone, sunblock, bottle of Evian.

5. **How do you refer to Association Football, i.e. what Man United and Celtic and them play?**
   a. Soccer.
   b. That foreign game! (*Accompanied by trembling and slavering at the mouth.*)
   c. Football. (*Real football then referred to as 'Gaelic'.*)

6. **Where is your preferred vantage point for the action?**
   a. Wedged underneath the scoreboard with 500 like-minded people, having the craic while trying not to pass out from a combination of the heat and a hangover that could sink a battleship.
   b. A good seat in the Hogan, up next to the bishop.
   c. Experiencing the game through a virtual reality full body suit in Holodeck 7 of the McCoca-Donald's corporate box … on the moon.

7. **What is the most common utterance to pass your lips during the hour?**
   a. 'Will ye get into them, for the love of fuck!'
   b. 'Pull on it, pull on it!'
   c. 'Watch your house, lads … Aw, come on, referee. That was never a penalty puck. Why didn't he consult with the fourth official?'

8. **What is the best treatment for a player whose head has been busted open by a wild hurley?**
   a. A slap on the face and some water poured on the wound from the magic bottle.

b. Arrah, he's grand, he's grand. He'll run it off.

c. You are unable to suggest anything as you've fainted at the sight of blood.

9. **What do you read between the minor and senior matches?**

   a. Nothing – you're too busy slagging off your buddies and getting psyched up for the 'big wan'.

   b. The programme from cover to cover, *Ireland on Sunday* (or whatever it's called now), your notes from the minor match.

   c. *The Observer*, the latest Chuck Palahniuk novel, the operating manual for your new Gizmotronic mobile phone with its own satellite dish and platinum aerial.

10. **What is your opinion of the national league?**

   a. 'The league's only a heap of ould shite, but it's a good laugh. And the pubs are never as packed afterwards either.'

   b. 'I haven't missed a league match since I contracted tuberculosis and nearly died … and even then my wife and the doctor had to tie me down to the bed.'

   c. 'The what?'

'Are you champ – or did you flop at the first round?'

You've searched your soul and dredged your memory banks; now here come the payback. Work out your score using the sophisticated testing system below.

Mostly As and Bs: You are the quintessential diehard – if you died any harder, you'd be dead already. Hey, it made sense when it first came to me. You are either a boorish ignoramus in a cowboy hat and too-tight jeans – living proof that alcohol really does kill brain cells – or an Olympic-level anal-retentive who needs to broaden their range of interests just a smidgen. Either way, you're one of the true servants of the association, you've been around for years and you'll stay around for ever, and we love ya.

Your fate: Life, so long as you keep going to matches.

Mostly Cs: Bzzz! Close, but no doughnut. You almost had everyone fooled there, but ultimately tripped yourself up with a few fatal mistakes. A crack team of all-in-one judge/jury/executioners noticed these little anomalies: Evian water? Holodeck 7? Fainting at the sight of blood pouring from a head wound!? Only a fake would have answered C to those ones. Hang your head in shame. Lower. No, lower again. Okay, that's low enough.

Your fate: Extermination!

KEEP THE FAITH

Ireland has become increasingly secular and materialistic in the past few decades, and the GAA has reflected that. Many people have long since swapped their rosary beads and peculiar certain-foods-on-certain-days rituals for astronomical house prices and a frankly absurd obsession with cooking. We're also, of course, an increasingly multi-denominational society, with people of all faiths and none living pious cheek by atheistic jowl.

So how to know the proper procedure if that new club member is a Jainist, Zoroastrian, Beelzebubian or Yugoslavian? How to avoid making an embarrassing or, in the case of that devil worshipper, potentially fatal gaffe about their religion? Here's a little guide to the world's major faiths, in terms you, the reader, will understand.

Catholicism: Belief in God guarantees victory – but you must feel guilty about it afterwards.

113

Presbyterianism: Hard work and sobriety will earn their just rewards (although the break of the ball could swing things either way).

Buddhism: The path to enlightenment is one of suffering – hence the maniacal training regimes now employed.

Islam: Allah will strike down the Yankee infidels (which might explain New York's consistently poor performances in the Connacht championship).

Taoism: Too complex to explain in one sentence.

Confucianism: Man who struggle on with hamstring injury in club match risk missing big inter-county final following week.

Judaism: We have wandered in the wilderness for forty years; God has forsaken us; we obviously need to put in more work at schools level.

Satanism: The Dark Lord will one day rise and bring Hell on earth – although after watching the average Ulster championship match, some believe this has already happened.

New Ageism: You have to feel the ley-line energy to truly be as one with the association (man).

Native American Animism: When I was a boy, my people ran freely over this half of the pitch. We had plentiful free space and many chances for goals. Where are those warriors now? They have been slaughtered by the hand-passing game.

Amish: What's sport?

Calvinism: The Damned and the Saved are pre-judged – so no amount of tinkering with the formats will help the weaker counties.

Moonies: Any chance we could use Croke Park for an upcoming mass wedding?

Hinduism: The caste system must be kept in place; we cannot have the pure mixing in the same division as the Untouchables (like Carlow).

114

Sikhism: These enormous plaits can be kinda hard to squeeze in under a helmet.

Evangelicalism: And on Judgement Day the Lord will smite down the wicked and those who brought in the backdoor system, sending them into the pits of Hell for interfering with the work of God and the traditional winner-takes-all structures. Testify!

The catechism of CLIChé

In his fantastic Myles na gCopaleen columns, Flann O'Brien would satirise the predictable, the trite and the meaningless through his hilarious Catecism of Cliché. And now you can use this handy reference guide to spot cliché usage at matches, meetings or in everyday conversation.

Of what is the club the cornerstone?
The entire association.

What prefix is invariably associated with the weaker counties?
So-called.

Of what is there none of that young fella at wing-forward?
Fear.

But what incorporeal part of him would a good scelp to the head soften?
His cough.

With what could his team-mate in the corner not hit a cow's arse at five paces?
A banjo.

With what was the man inside him thick last night, a situation consequently hampering his performance today?
The drink.

How much short of a tramp is that referee?
Nothing.

And what does he need to get checked pronto?
His glasses.

What would that big horse of a man at midfield do to a brick wall for you?
Go through it.

Because he is built like what other sort of brick structure?
A shite-house.

In what direction will this selfless fellow bust the play, to the advantage of his team-mates?
Up.

What is the most desired quality in a corner-back?
Stickiness.

And a half-back?
Knackiness.

And a half-forward?
The propensity to take flight.

And a corner-forward?
Deadliness.

Off what is the dressing-room door normally left hanging?
The hinges.

Off what do craggy old full-backs deliver the majority of digs to their markers?
The ball.

By what term is this sort of happening usually referred to?
An incident.

What part of the team's individual bodies had the trainer run off them the other night?
The legs.

Because he is a what for the physical stuff?
Savage.

The media

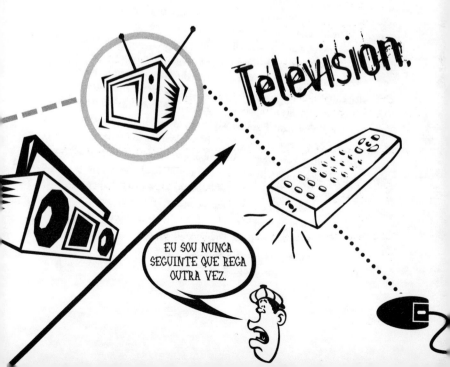

Under **press**-ure

Renowned communications theorist Marshall McLuhan contended, 'The medium is the message.' Post-modern philosopher Jean Baudrillard claimed that the media symbol has become partly constitutive of the reality it represents. And Cyril Farrell once famously – and nonsensically – declared, 'That's why they call him Santy, Ger.'

Ah, yes. The media is/are a powerful thing/things (never could figure out whether that was a single or plural noun). And nowhere more so than in GAA, where a trenchant observation or withering putdown by one of our fine members of the press can throw even the greatest player's qualities into doubt. Such is the authority we wield (please note: authority wielded in stringently fair and benevolent manner at all times). As far back as 1910, one florid stylist was bemoaning the demise in Cavan football fortunes, declaiming, 'You can't cut finished footballers out of a hedge. Muscle in the county is running wild for want of cultivation.' Ooh, hark at Lord Byron himself. 'Running wild for want of cultivation,' no less.

The life of a GAA hack is a good one, and not just because it enables you to stretch adolescence well into middle age. Liquid breakfasts in ratty pubs with INLA links, slugging back pints while subtly ogling the girl who collects the glasses ... sure, who wouldn't want to do it? It also facilitates free entry into many sporting events, commands much respect from the sad sacks you went to school with, and has a certain '1940s *film noir* New York on a rainy night' sexiness. Well, rainy afternoon in Edenderry, anyway.

And press coverage of the GAA has exploded in recent decades, a far cry from the dark past when some Dublin newspaper proprietors effectively ignored the country's biggest cultural movement because of its perceived links to faction-fighting and republicanism, and actual links to uncool bog-trotter types who just didn't fit that coveted ABC1 demographic. But such ignorance and prejudice has thankfully abated, mainly because many uncool bog-trotter types moved up to Dublin and now run the place. Ha, ha!

The national papers, in the same time, have moved away from straight-forward reportage and quotes. Games used to be described purely in terms of scores recorded, which was slightly more boring than listening to shortwave radio static for ten hours, though significantly less boring than listening to an FM radio station for ten minutes. Like so: 'Clare were first off the mark with a point after two minutes. Limerick replied with a point of their own. Then they scored two more points to lead by three points to one. Then Clare replied with a goal. Then Limerick hit two wides. Then my heart went into seizure and I lost all will to live. Then I watched the grass grow for a while. Then something else happened. At half-time it was still all to play for.'

Con Houlihan was always there, ploughing his unique furrow, but generally the copy was staid, sombre and stuck rigidly to the facts. In short, a load of crapola. But that's all in the past, and we now have columns from ex-players and managers, cutesy little coloured graphs, the fans' perspective, and Vincent Hogan's sparkling use of metaphor and extended metaphor. One can even read a review of the sporting telly if, for some bizarre reason, one would choose to. (Projected future pieces: the top-ten action replays, the Pulitzer Bland Analysis Award, and your chance to vote on the Most Hilarious Commentating Cock-Up of the Decade.)

But the greatest indicator of change is the appearance of the 'funny' piece, which takes an affectionately acerbic look at some quirk or other of the GAA scene. They lampoon and pay homage in equal measure, written by someone with a genuine love for GAA but who also finds it funny to point and laugh, the perfect mix of smart-ass and soft-hearted.

Damn. If only *I'd* thought of doing that.

Of course, the provincial papers also devote smudgy acres of their publications to coverage of the GAA 'scene', which is understandable enough when you consider that hardly anything interesting ever happens in most places. It's true, you know it is. The writing, particularly on local issues, tends to be pretty cautious, which again is understandable given that the dude at the typewriter could be a cousin of the manager, or the full-foward delivers his coal and he doesn't want it dumped on top of his car some morning. They do get to throw off the shackles a bit when discussing inter-county, however, where no position is too blinkered or utterance too rash, especially if said utterance refers to a particularly hated player from a neighbouring county. In fact, this will often result in a hefty raise.

The Festertown
Chronicle

A standard-bearer for local newspapers • Annoying our neighbours in Knocknaglockoff since 1952

Printed in a big factory somewhere outside Dundalk   *Price €4.75 (excl. VAT)*

Man Plays On Without Head

Corner-forward praised for 'immense bravery'
By Dutch Mastourakis,
Chief Sports Reporter

Veteran Festertown corner-forward Belgo 'The Hammer' McFeeley earned further acclaim on Saturday evening when he finished a match despite losing his head after forty-five minutes of play. McFeeley was decapitated midway through the second-half of a hurling challenge against St Sebastian of the Woeful Visions Gaels.

McFeeley was decapitated midway through the second half

The incident occurred when Belgo, known to friends as 'The Belgian', leapt up for a high ball on the edge of the square. Apparently, he hit the opposition full-back 'a right dunt' in the ribs, who retaliated by screwing off the top of his hurley to reveal an authentic Samurai sword. This was then used to slice McFeeley's head from his shoulders.

The severed head rolled over the line, leading to some confusion as to whether or not a goal had been scored. Eventually, the referee decided it had not, and awarded a throw-in on the St Sebastian's 14-yard line. The full-back was given a yellow card, for 'ungentlemanly and undeniably life-threatening conduct'.

McFeeley waved off medical help and continued to play. The fact ▶

that he was running around like a headless chicken – quite literally – was merely a slight hindrance as he scored a point and set up a teammate for the winning goal.

Speaking to the *Chronicle* later from a bucket of ice on the clubhouse bar counter, his head explained, 'Basically, they propped me up on the bonnet of a car so I could see what was going on. I then shouted out instructions to my body – turn left, pull on it, rap his knuckles, whatever. It all worked out fairly well, thank God.'

Honorary club president, Fr Ignatious Polaroid SJ, paid tribute to a remarkable performance, prais-

> **'Basically, they propped me up on the bonnet of a car so I could see what was going on.'**

ing Belgo's courage and surprisingly good co-ordination considering. McFeeley modestly declined such praise, remarking, 'To be honest, the important thing at the end of the day is that the team won, and that's just what we done. Whether the scores come from my headless body or one of the other lads doesn't matter. It's a team effort, and we'll all look at the video for the next day.'

An uncomfortable silence then followed when it was pointed out to McFeeley that he couldn't watch the video for the next day, as his head now resided in a cryogenic freezing chamber in Arizona, next to Walt Disney's.

End This Madness!

Club chairman slams situation at AGM

Long-serving Festertown Mashers chairman, Binky Shine, recently slammed new developments at a slap-up chicken and ham supper in the Mashers' newly refurbished clubhouse, Klubb Monty Carlow. Shine, known as 'The Shiner' to family and close associates, but not to people who don't like him (who refer to him as 'The Fat Fool'), made several incendiary remarks about certain innovations just passed at Congress.

Shine was in such a rabid state by the end of his speech that his wife had to hold on to his fetching toupee to keep it attached to his head. This endeared him even further to the capacity crowd which cheered him on like a fevered mob, a bit like what you might find attacking Castle Frankenstein with pitchforks.

Speaking too loudly into a mistuned microphone, Shine blasted, 'This madness must end. For too ▶

long we have put up with the big-wigs in the crow's nest trying to tell us what to do. Well, I'm a member of this great association and, in my book, being a member of something doesn't mean having to follow rules! We must stand up for our rights! We must shout stop!'

When reasonable-minded club treasurer, local primary teacher Liam Mac Liaim, asked to which developments exactly Shine was referring, he was roundly booed and pelted with egg salad sandwiches. The evening ended with a late bar and karaoke session, during which Shine sang 'Pretty Little Girl from Omagh' and 'I Will Survive' by Gloria Gaynor.

Deaths Notices

Phil 'Philip' Curley, died aged fifty-one on 19 July of a heart attack while watching a minor match. Sorely missed by his many friends at Festertown Mashers and all at the Dirty Sailor pub, where he spent most of his money. 'He died the way he would have wanted – roaring abuse at a linesman.' **RIP.**

Télévision,

drug of the nation(al games)

In many instances of innovation and progress – line dancing, the jogging craze, remote-controlled warfare – America has led the way. And thus it was with television, for the first GAA match to be televised was a hurling tie in Gaelic Park, New York, in 1951. But, as usual, it didn't take long for the Paddies to catch on that this cathode ray thingie had certain plus points, such as its ability to beam footage of matches into the fourteen Irish homes that then possessed a television set.

When Telefís Éireann was set up in 1961, the legendary Micheál O'Hehir was made head of sport, and TV rights for the All-Ireland finals, semi-finals and Railway Cup finals were secured from the GAA at the ridiculous, weren't-things-much-cheaper-back-then cost of £10. (Though the Railway Cup is probably still available for about a tenski.) Since then, it's been onwards, upwards and inwards (to our frontal lobes) for the monster in the corner, with scores of matches now shown live each year, DVD compilations an annual lifesaver for unimaginative Christmas-gift buyers, and the mangulation of both the English language and logical thought turned into an art form by our venerable studio analysts.

Though the so-called 'independent' station TV3 has resolutely ignored GAA for much of its existence, TG4 has done sterling work in broadcasting the matches that RTÉ often couldn't be bothered with: women's football, county finals, provincial club championships, colleges stuff. As well as shining a light on the lesser-spotted fauna of our Gaelic ecosystem, this also helps couch potatoes brush up on their command of the native tongue, which is obviously *rud maith*. (You see? It's working already!) And the likes of *Breaking Ball*, *BBX* and *Park Live* have represented a little of the fun, broader culture and outright daftness of GAA, with varying success.

But the daddy of them all, of course, is *The Sunday Game*, RTÉ's flagship summer show since 1979. For most of us, this is now as much a part of the Lord's Day as glutinous dinners, buying too many newspapers and dodging mass. Okay, so I will concede that the programme's kind of lame sometimes, and the analysis can be incredibly bland, and the graphics are a bit dated, and Colm O'Rourke makes me want to violently devolve the set into its constituent parts. But there's something sort of comforting about *The Sunday Game*, like a scruffy old dog that doesn't really do anything but lie around the kitchen all day, and you just can't help developing a fondness for the poor dumb critter.

It also seems to suit the games a little better, this vaguely ramshackle approach, in thankful contrast to the flashy, Jerry Bruckheimer-production style of Sky Sports *et al*. And with sports this dramatic and exciting, who needs flamboyant graphics and hyperventilating sidekicks? Michael Lyster has also come into his own as an amiable, relaxed (and subtly witty) host. For good or bad, the programme has become as big a fixture of match day as recklessly purchasing unhygienic burgers from roadside vans. And, ultimately, it's just television, folks. If you don't like it, go read a book instead.

Now, if only they hadn't arsed around with that iconic theme music …

'Do You Feel Loved?' – U2

'Get Off' – Dandy Warhols

'Flower Duet' from *Lakmé* – Delibes

We lost that one in translation, Marty

> Fußball war der wirkliche Sieger.

> Teníamos un punto a probar hoy y lo probamos.

> Conduisez-le dans le bas.

What with our growing richness, desire for new experiences and belated realisation that we're being royally screwed by every greasy till-fumbler in the country, holidays abroad have never been more popular with GAA fans. Sun, sea, sangría and fat English yobs with the cross of St George tattooed on their capacious bellies – what could be finer?

You can also, in most places, now watch all the Gaelic games action as it is broadcast on satellite TV. But what if – for some strange and, now that I think of it, not very likely reason – the commentary is in a foreign tongue? Or if you don't want to break the exotic idyll by hollering abuse at the screen in boring old English? Well, now you don't have to. Simply remember these key phrases, in a variety of commonly used European languages, and make that summer break even more special. →

The best **Sunday Game** end-of-show montage musical accompaniments ♪♫♪

'Time to Say Goodbye' –
Sarah Brightman and Andrea Bocelli

Something pretty groovy by David Holmes

'Push It' –
Garbage

'Right Here, Right Now' –
Fatboy Slim

125

SPANISH

Will ye get into them!
¡Voluntad que usted consigue en ellos!

We had a point to prove today … and we proved it.
Teníamos un punto a probar hoy y lo probamos.

Cork will have another look at the video tonight and see where they went wrong.
El Cork tendrá otra mirada en el vídeo esta noche y vio adónde fueron mal.

GERMAN

Football was the real winner.
Fußball war der wirkliche Sieger.

Talk us through Limerick's first goal there, Tomás.
Sprechen Sie uns durch Limerick erstes Ziel dort, Tomás.

They knew they had a job to do and that's exactly what they done.
Sie kannten sie hatten einen Job zu tun und das ist genau, was sie getan.

ITALIAN

What's Spillane saying now?
Che cosa Spillane ora sta dicendo?

He's nothing short of a tramp.
È niente ma un vagabondo.

The GAA needs a strong Dublin team.
Il GAA ha bisogno di una squadra forte de Dublino.

It's wonderful to see all the boys and girls here today in their colours.
È meraviglioso vedere tutti i ragazzi e ragazze qui oggi nei loro colori.

EU SOU NUNCA SEGUINTE QUE REGA OUTRA VEZ.

Che cosa Spillane ora sta dicendo?

PORTUGUESE

Keep the high balls low and the wides to a minimum.
Mantenha as esferas elevadas baixos e os wides a um mínimo.

Later on in the programme, we'll have highlights of the O'Byrne Cup final.
Mais tarde sobre no programa, n's teremos destaques do final do Copo de O'Byrne.

I'm never following that shower again.
Eu sou nunca seguinte que rega outra vez.

FRENCH

Drive it in low.
Conduisez–le dans le bas.

Look after the points and let the goals look after themselves.
Occupez–vous des points et laissez les buts s'occuper.

Pull on it, for the love of Jesus!
Tirez là–dessus, pour l'amour de Jésus!

I love you, Cyril, and I want to have your babies.
Je t'aime, Cyril, et je veux avoir tes enfants.

I never made any promises

Don't put your house on it – five predictions that went slightly awry.

1 'Tyrone will never win an All-Ireland with Brian Dooher in the team.' **Colm O'Rourke**

2 'Offaly will never win an All-Ireland unless they do things my way.' **Babs Keating**

3 'Cuba will be submerged beneath the Atlantic as a punishment by God.' **David Icke**

4 'Man will have developed interstellar and time travel by 1987.' **Buck Rogers**

5 'Man will have developed interstellar and time travel by yesterday.' **Me**

TV GAA-GAA

10 a.m. **A Chairde – An Urbi agus An Orbi**
Papal address from the balcony of St Peter's Basilica on increased ecumenism, the place of faith in the modern world, and the difficulties in finding a trustworthy young fella to man the scoreboard during schools matches. ★

10.30 a.m. **FILM: All Quiet on the Western Front**
Classic anti-war movie, telling the sad tale of a group of Connacht footballers who realise the source of an eerie silence to be the rest of the country gone to Croke Park for the All-Ireland final, leaving them behind in their own personal hell.
Idealistic young squaddie –
CONOR MORTIMER
Grizzled sergeant –
JOHN MAUGHAN
Sweetheart left at home –
ANY ONE OF THE TG4
WEATHERGIRLS
Lord Kitchener –
DANNY LYNCH
Director Orson Welles (1937)
Subtitles 666 ★★★

12.15 p.m. **Aussiemaniacs**
Cartoon fun with the loveable – not to mention terrifying – scamps from Down Under as they wreak comedic destruction on their International Rules opponents' heads. ★★★

12.45 p.m. **The Sunday Game Special: 'Don't Quote Me On That'**
Michael Lyster, backed by an eclectic musical selection, introduces a montage of the best of the season's punditry, including: Pat Spillane visibly teeing up a joke at least fifteen minutes before making it; Tom Mulcahy hedging his bets; and a little-seen but surprisingly heated spat between Cyril Farrell and Kevin McStay on which is the better game. ★★★★

1.45 p.m. **FILM: Carlow Jones and the Temple of Doom**
Intrepid archaeologist and hurling fan Dr Carlow Jones risks life and olfactory senses by braving the feared 'Temple of Doom' – or 'Fir' in

the natives' language –
at Fraher's Field while
searching for the Golden
Hoop of Dungarvan. Can
Carlow escape before the
cunningly booby-trapped
urinal overpowers him…?
Dr Carlow Jones –
BRIAN 'BEANO' MCDONALD
Rival archaeologist –
RONAN CLARKE
Keeper of a Dark Secret –
RANDOM UNHELPFUL
COUNTY BOARD PRO
Carlow's Dad –
SEAN CONNERY
Director Steven Spielberg
(1984) Subtitles 24-7 ★★

3.40 p.m. **The Bolshoi Ballet at Croke Park**

Pick of the Day
Russia's legendary ballet
troupe performs various
twirls, whirls and pirouettes
to the accompaniment of the
Artane Boys' Band during
half-time of the All-Ireland
U16 B hurling semi-final
between Tyrone and Leitrim.
Includes music from La
Sylphide, The Nutcracker
Suite and Take Me Home to
Mayo. Conductor: Herbert
O'Karajan. ★★★★★

5.40 p.m. **News**
Frank Lohan presents a
round-up of all the day's
major world events, with
analysis and comment by
the entire Kilmacud Crokes

squad. Followed by financial
news with Paul Galvin.

6.00 p.m. **FILM:** **The Postman Doesn't Always Ring Twice**
Steamy thriller about a rabid
Kilkenny fan who loses out
on his All-Ireland final tickets
because he's in the shower
when the postman arrives,
sparking off a homicidal
rampage in the Canal End
during the minor match. Only
one obsessed Maor can
bring him down…
Kilkenny fan –
JACK NICHOLSON
Obsessed Maor – AL PACINO
Sultry femme fatale –
LAUREN BACALL
The Postman – POSTMAN PAT
Director Brian De Palma
(1992) Subtitles 4-7-11
★★★

7.50 p.m. **Tired Old Retread of Previously Shown Cabaret**
TV GAA-GAA wheels out a
host of depressingly
predictable faces for an
all-singing, all-dancing,
all-crap extravaganza. Some
generic boyband members
embarrass themselves by
attempting to learn hurling,
Sonny Knowles does that
silly hand-waving thing with
four disinterested-looking
Monaghan supporters,
while Paul Durcan gives a

heartrending recital of classic GAA match report, 'Wicklow Rue Missed Chances as Wexford Snatch Late Draw'. ★

9.30 p.m. **FILM: Butterfingers**
Lesser-known Bond movie sees James facing his toughest test – a chronic attack of jittery hands on the eve of a big handball match against the top Soviet contender to decide how to carve up Eastern Europe. His co-ordination deserting him, the future of the free world at stake and his favourite singlet lying dirty in the laundry basket, can the dapper superspy/handballer prevail?
James Bond – TONY DAVIS
Evil Soviet handballer –
YURICHENKO
DEWHEELFELLOV
M – LIAM GRIFFIN
Match referee –
PAT McENEANEY
Director Cubby Broccoli
(1972)
Subtitles 007 ★★★

11.15 p.m. **A Prediction at Bedtime**
Contemplative spiritual programme whereby an expert panel gives its predictions on what will happen throughout the course of the night and the following day. Sombre, moving voiceover: Ger Canning. ★★

11.20 p.m. **FILM: Hurley Scoop**
Wittily titled, anarchic comedy starring Chevy Chase as intrepid investigative GAA reporter, Ernest 'Scoop' McAdoo. Whilst covering a routine county convention in Laois, Scoop stumbles upon a conspiracy to force through changes to the tackle rule which could make some people very rich – and Scoop very dead…
Ernest 'Scoop' McAdoo –
CHEVY CHASE
County Chairman –
BRIAN DENNEHY
Gruff but soft-hearted newspaper editor –
PAUL NEWMAN
Convention caterer –
AINSLEY HARRIOTT
Director Mel Brooks (1986)
Subtitles 10-4 ★★★

RATINGS

★★★★★	**Fantabulacious**
★★★★	**Smokin' Hot**
★★★	**'S'All Right**
★★	**Maggoty**
★	**Kill Me Now**

Who wants to b€ a
MILLIONAIRE?*

You do! Or you should, anyway. Unless you're already fabulously rich, in which case can I have a loan of two hundred quid? I'm good for it, honest. I just need it for a new bike for the young fella.

Anyway, this is your ideal chance to win not a hundred – not a thousand – but ONE MILLION imaginary euro! Tax free! And like in the formerly quite popular gameshow, all you have to do is answer a series of increasingly preposterous questions on All-Ireland finals, ranging from pathetically easy to impossibly difficult, to bag the big prize. Now it's straight over to your host, a picture of Marty Morrissey.

Take it away!

Sitting comfortably? Here is your starter for 1,000 imaginary euro:
What is the name of the cup what is won by the All-Ireland hurling champions?
A. The FA Cup.
B. The Holy Grail.
C. The Liam MacCarthy.
D. A big cup of tea.

For 2,000 imaginary euro:
Who scored Meath's goal in the 1999 football final?
A. Mick Lyons.
B. Navan Man.
C. Thomas the Tank Engine.
D. Ollie Murphy.

For 4,000 imaginary euro:
Which Kerry player cheekily chipped the ball over Paddy Cullen in the 1978 football final?
A. Mikey Sheehy.
B. A cheeky monkey.
C. Charlie Nelligan.
D. Aeroplane O'Shea.

131

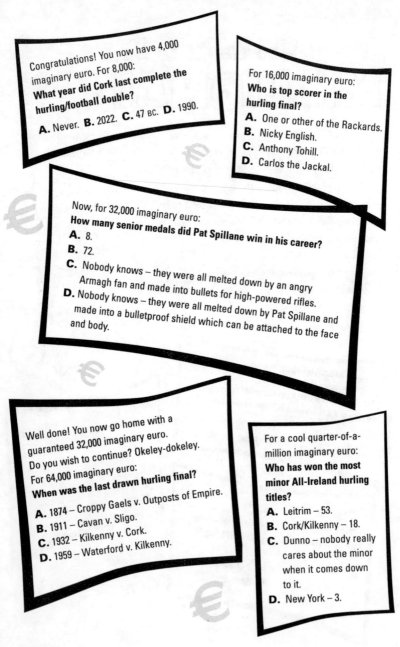

Congratulations! You now have 4,000 imaginary euro. For 8,000:
What year did Cork last complete the hurling/football double?

A. Never. **B.** 2022. **C.** 47 BC. **D.** 1990.

For 16,000 imaginary euro:
Who is top scorer in the hurling final?
A. One or other of the Rackards.
B. Nicky English.
C. Anthony Tohill.
D. Carlos the Jackal.

Now, for 32,000 imaginary euro:
How many senior medals did Pat Spillane win in his career?
A. 8.
B. 72.
C. Nobody knows – they were all melted down by an angry Armagh fan and made into bullets for high-powered rifles.
D. Nobody knows – they were all melted down by Pat Spillane and made into a bulletproof shield which can be attached to the face and body.

Well done! You now go home with a guaranteed 32,000 imaginary euro. Do you wish to continue? Okeley-dokeley.
For 64,000 imaginary euro:
When was the last drawn hurling final?

A. 1874 – Croppy Gaels v. Outposts of Empire.
B. 1911 – Cavan v. Sligo.
C. 1932 – Kilkenny v. Cork.
D. 1959 – Waterford v. Kilkenny.

For a cool quarter-of-a-million imaginary euro:
Who has won the most minor All-Ireland hurling titles?
A. Leitrim – 53.
B. Cork/Kilkenny – 18.
C. Dunno – nobody really cares about the minor when it comes down to it.
D. New York – 3.

For a humongous half-a-million imaginary euro:

What was unusual about Charlie Redmond's sending-off in the 1995 final?

A. He was sent off for wearing a tutu and dancing parts of *Swan Lake* during half-time.

B. He was sent off but remained on the field for about five minutes before being spotted.

C. The referee sent him off by speaking in iambic pentameter.

D. He sent the referee off, then awarded himself a penalty. Which he missed.

Congratulations! You are now just one question away from being an imaginary millionaire! Nervous? Confident? Whatever – I'm just here to ask the questions. So – for that perfect million squids – your final question:

What was the gate receipt for the 1896 football final in which Limerick beat Dublin?

A. £101, 1 shilling, no pence.

B. 26 shekels.

C. A leprechaun's crock of gold, two sheep in good health and the blood of an Englishman.

D. Limerick beat Dublin!? Get out of here!

Answers – C, D, A, D, B, A, D, C, B, A

Before you came here, you had nothing. But now - if you answered A - you've done it! You are an imaginary millionaire! Congratulations! You are free to go and spend that money - not wisely but too well. Now - about that few hundred quid...?

*Not affiliated in any way with the real *Who Wants To Be A Millionaire?*, Marty Morrissey, the cathode-ray tube or the making of any money whatsoever.

133

A Star is Born

The All-Stars as we know them today began in 1971, though different papers and magazines had sporadically published teams before that. Interestingly, one of the early sponsors was Carroll's cigarettes, which may explain why fitness levels were noticeably lower in olden days. It's hard to yomp up the MacGillicuddy Reeks when your lungs are coated in about two inches of dense, black tar.

Anyway, the new awards soon caught fire in the public imagination, with the annual announcement of teams giving GAA fans a chance to do what we love best – complain. The standard post-ceremony reaction goes something along these lines: 'How the hell did (Player A) not get picked? It's only because (Player B) didn't get one last year and they wanted to make it up to him. And why were there so many picked from (Team Z)? They wouldn't have any if they hadn't won (Competition F). And I cannot believe (Player C) won another one, the useless bast—'

But there are other reasons why we love the All-Stars. The sight of ninety brawny men dolled up in tuxedos is always amusing, as are those deliciously embarrassing moments when a guy with a microphone puts pointless

★★★

WHY IS IT THAT...?
With Professor Salman MacDripsey M.Phil.

Readers: Do you have a query about GAA nagging at your brain since, ooh, ten minutes ago? A friendly debate about some finer point of the game threatening to escalate into bloody conflict? Let *The Festertown Chronicle*'s erudite agony aunt/uncle sort it out.

★★★★★★★★★★★★★★★★★★★★★★★★★★★★★★

questions to people who clearly don't want to answer. And I have very fond memories of the free posters they gave out to primary schools in the 1970s, replete with mugshots so unflattering they looked like a collection of America's Most Wanted. With added moustaches.

Still, I feel the ceremony itself could do with jazzing up. It's the twenty-first century, people! They need a good dose of pep, a big mother of a needle full of pizazz jammed straight into the brain. So why not poach the best of other awards ceremonies to form a new All-Stars super-ceremony? Keep the fundamental point of the competition (rewarding great deeds on the field) but in MTV- and Oscar-style categories. So we could have Best Supporting Act (such-and-such an unheralded mullocker who 'busts up the play'), Most Popular Act (whichever minnow has crawled out of the swamp of failure that year), and the first Free Your Mind award (dedicated to fáinne-wearing mohair suits everywhere).

But the most crucial part is the presentation. So instead of Ger and Marty in the Burlo, what's wrong with Manumission in Ibiza? Why not invite funny-faced Justin Timberlake to present the Player of the Year award in his underwear? Or how about Christina Aguilera handing over the goalkeeping gong in *her* underwear? That'd increase viewer figures for sure. And I'm amazed it's never occurred to anyone to stage a musical spectacular based on the Ulster final, starring one or other of McFly as the Armagh centre-back, Norah Jones as an umpire and Cate Blanchett as the entire Down support (she's very versatile).

That would also increase viewing … actually, no, it probably wouldn't. But we won't let that stop us.

★★★★★★★★★★★★★★★★★★★★★★★★★★★★★★★★★

Why is it that … players who were fit enough to come on as a sub weren't fit enough to start? *Stanislaus Gaylord, Louth*
The Prof says: Good question, Stan, and one I'm delighted you 'axed'. If a player has been injured for, let's say, a month, but has just recovered fitness, he's now fit enough to play, but due to a lack of training won't have the stamina to last the full hour. Hence his introduction as a sub when the game is already lost and it's too late to do anything about it anyway.

Why is it that … soccer togs keep changing from castratingly tight to ridiculously enormous and back, while GAA togs have remained the same? *Irwin Kirwan, Westmeath*
The Prof says: Hmm … quite a teaser there, Irwin. By the way, is that actually your real name? I have my doubts. Anyway, you're not quite accurate when you say GAA togs haven't changed – I personally remember needing butter and a crowbar to wedge myself into my skimpy acrylic shorts in the 1970s.

YOU LOVE ME, YOU REALLY LOVE ME

**'I dedicate this to the linesman at last year's U11 semi-final.'
Three other awards the All-Stars could steal a trick from.**

THE OSCARS: The flash of cameras and grovelling of sycophants are all forgotten as Sally Field breaks down on receiving the statuette for corner-forward.

THE MAN BOOKER: Limited to a small geographical area, this two-bit prize always goes to the most ungrammatical player (a tough choice, admittedly).

THE TURNER PRIZE: Prestigious award for excellence in the field of controversial, confrontational art. Last year's winner bottled the blood spilled at the Tyrone county final and displayed it as a commentary on the random violence of modern life.

Why is it that … when a point is scored, the umpire who isn't in possession of the flag always leans back really far, pauses for effect and then dramatically points at his buddy to raise the flag? *Fionnuala Banshee, The Top of a Mountain*
The Prof says: Ah – the classic case of insane envy manifesting itself as stealing your comrade's thunder; or, to give it its technical term, 'stealing your comrade's thunder'. The almost total lack of goals in the modern game have left the 'green flag' man feeling a little left out. But plans are afoot to equip them with handheld Tetris games to keep them amused.

Why is it that … the sliotar has those funny rims around the side? Is it for aero-dynamics or what? *Benjamin Franklin (Baaaaw), Elementary School*
The Prof says: I've rooted through my extensive collection of nudie magaz— … um, GAA history books, and the only reference I could find came from an old report on the Tailteann Games of 1573 BC. 'And the Chieftain didst find himself displeased when a slippery ball made him miss a vital penalty; and yea, he didst order the skinning of a fatted calf and its skin to be placeth on the ball in a sort of squiggly pattern. And so it was written and came to pass and all that.'

RADIO HEADS

The very first radio broadcast of field sports anywhere in Europe happened in 1926, when Galway and Kilkenny's All-Ireland hurling semi-final was covered by the nascent Irish service, 2RN. And if that doesn't make your heart swell with patriotic pride, then you, sir or madam, have no heart to swell.

Radio may have been swiftly overtaken in the glamour stakes by its younger sibling, TV, but it has remained a hugely popular, and hugely powerful, medium. RTÉ has always proven itself a true friend of the GAA, with extensive coverage throughout the year … and I say this as someone who used to be driven to near-homicidal mania by Brian Carthy's habit of mentioning D.J. Carey in every match commentary, regardless of who was playing. Seán Óg Ó Ceallacháin's Sunday night results round-up is an institution. And with the advent of local stations in recent decades, radio's role in promoting Gaelic games has never been greater.

Why is it that … they stopped putting a big flashing 'R' on the telly when a replay would be shown? I used love that big old 'R'. It was great. They won't tell me anything in here. They say I've to stay in a padded room all by myself. It's not fair.
Napoleon Bonaparte, Electroshock Ward, Kilmarnock Institute for the Dangerously Deranged
The Prof says: Ah, Napoleon, I share your pain. I, too, used admire greatly that big flashing 'R' what they had on telly for a replay. But progress can't be stopped, and it was discarded at the end of the seventies for being 'too seventies', and because it reminded everyone of horrible huge frizzy hair. Like Patrick Duffy's in *Dallas*. It was replaced by a sort of rectangle that swooshed into view.

Why is it that … summers used always be hotter years ago? I think they used, anyway.
Peats Dribble, The Far Side of the Moon (the bit that isn't made out of cheese)
The Prof says: Unfortunately, Peats, I am unable to answer your question as I am bound by various fraudulent advertising regulations to only address queries directly related to Gaelic games. However, I did refer to my good friend, Doctor Horst Bendix of the Munchausen Institute for Experimentation on the Lunatic, who fancies himself a bit of an expert on these things. He declared: 'The sun? Yeah, the sun used to be hotter, all right. That's 'cause of all the pollution and stuff – it's formed a kind of 'umbrella' over the world, stopping the heat from reaching us. So wrap up well, kids.'

The most famous Irish radio (and television) commentator, of course, was Micheál O'Hehir, who did his first stint at the mike as a raw eighteen-year-old in 1938. Oddly, he didn't become a full-time commentator for another twenty-one years, instead working in the civil service. What, were budgets really so tight back then? O'Hehir's successor as the voice of the GAA airwaves is the formidable Micheál Ó Muircheartaigh, whose loquacious, almost Wagnerian commentaries have become imperative for many stay-at-home fans and have provided hundreds of amusing quotes for bored corporate drones to email to each other in an endless cycle of ineffectiveness.

On a historical tangent, the BBC's Belfast station 2BE introduced sports results to its Sunday news in 1934. However, the bastard statelet's prime minister, some twat called Lord Craigavon, insisted that GAA results be dropped because they were 'hurting the feelings of the majority of the people'. Hurting their *feelings*? I'm sorry, I didn't realise that gerrymandering, imperialist, sectarian, quasi-Aryan supremacists actually had feelings to hurt.

Sadly, these shameful attitudes still persist, with certain Irish radio stations insisting on blanket coverage of their beloved English Premiership soccer while treating our national sports as some sort of cute provincial curiosity. Ah, fuck 'em and feed 'em Froot Loops. That's the best thing about radio: you can always turn the dial.

● ●

Why is it that … you never see those faceguard helmets that looked like the packaging for a stereo system any more? Now they all look like skateboard helmets or something. What was wrong with those big boxy ones? If it worked for Volvos, it can work for hurling. *Lestat the Vampire, eighteenth-century France*
The Prof says: The reason, my dear Lestat, is very simple. Players found that the old 'rectangulocentric paralleloid infrastructure' – or 'box' – hindered their vision, and also made them look like total dorks. Thus the new 'heliocentric orbitular radial exoskeleton' – or 'curved' – look came in. Now they all look like killer cyborgs from *Battlestar Galactica*.

Why is it that … the Sam Maguire has only two handles, while the Liam MacCarthy has four? Are they codding us? *Albert Camus, Algiers*
The Prof says: There are two schools of thought on this. One contends that because footballers are generally beefier men, it only takes one to lift the cup, whereas hurlers, being slighter and skinnier, require two sets of hands. The other maintains that there were originally four handles on Sam, but they were knocked off during some overly enthusiastic celebrations in the North during the mid-1990s. Ah, but you can't blame them, really.

Board game

If there's one thing that defines the average GAA fan, it is our love of discussion. In many ways, following a team is meaningless without the pre-, post- and during-match analysis and debate. Playing a game is one thing, but following a sport from the (metaphorical or otherwise) sidelines – *sin scéal eile*.

Imagine how boring and vaguely pointless it would be if we travelled to matches, cheered the team in isolation, went home and watched reruns on video. Conversations would become stilted to the point of embarrassment when one fellow would ask his friend, 'Did you see the game?' and receive the reply, 'Yes. Yes, I did,' followed by some conspicuously uncomfortable whistling.

Chatting about Gaelic games, then, is a pivotal part of the whole endeavour. And with the advent of internet discussion boards, we need no longer restrict ourselves to debating the issues on the phone, the bus or the chiropractor's surgery table. ➡

Why is it that … people are allowed wear those ridiculous straw cowboy hats to matches? Surely Central Council should put a ban on them? *Coco Chanel, Paris*
The Prof says: There actually was a ban on the wearing of straw cowboy hats under the contentious Rule 94 which was introduced in 1951. It stated, 'Any member of Cumann Lúthcleas Gael witnessed in this headgear will be banned from playing, mentoring or rabidly following any or all GAA teams and matches for the foreseeable future. Actually, no, make that for ever and ever, to infinity and beyond, until the end of time when the sun is extinguished and the earth ceases to exist.' However, the ban was overturned on appeal.

➡

The GAA is now floating around cyberspace, for everyone from office clock-punchers to paranoid survivalists in Montana to access, and there is potentially an infinity of discussion boards out there – in theory, every single personal page devoted to one's county or club could include its own board. In actuality, four or five (anfearrua, gaaboard, premierview, rebelgaa, hill16 – appy polly loggys if I've left yours out) have the minimum required complement of souls contributing, and are thus worth reading. The rest are either in permanent 'under construction' limbo, or the online equivalent of a ghost town, where one half expects to see digital tumbleweed drifting slowly across the screen as the eerie sound of a howling wind escapes from your speakers. Still, if the denizens of other sites are getting on your nerves, these make for an ideal retreat.

Finally, please be advised that any or all of these sites may have been consumed alive by a murderous virus of Singaporean origin since the time of writing/reading this book. The author and publishers accept no responsibility for consequent disappointment.

Why is it that ... you never see sight nor sound of the bottleman any more? That fella was doctor, priest and best friend all in one, and could wash away all your troubles with a slug from the magic bottle. And I loved our local bottleman like I've never loved another man before.
Ted Castle, somewhere in the late 1970s
The Prof says: *Riiight.* Uh, some salient points there, Ted. However, I think you'll find that having trained medical people on the sideline proved slightly more efficacious than an untrained bag-carrier who believed a gaping wound would miraculously heal itself after application of plain tap water. You weirdo.

He said **WHAT!?**

A few words of warning

★ Irish people are notorious for our ability, and ever-ready willingness, to swear in mindbogglingly inventive ways. If you're of a delicate disposition, therefore, maybe discussion boards aren't the place for you.

★ Be prepared to have your opinions and arguments attacked on all sides. But don't get too precious about it: it's only harmless banter, and arguing is kind of the point.

★ Don't give out personal information and don't try to wheedle this out of others. Anonymity is sacrosanct and, anyway, using a nickname allows people to behave in ways they might never normally. Woody Allen becomes Conan the Destroyer online.

★ Unless you're of a masochistic bent, strictly avoid most Irish discussion boards dedicated to rival sports. The ill-informed opinions of cretinous anti-GAA bozos about Croke Park, Rule 42, payment for players and other such topics are scary.

● ●

Ted replies: It would! Sure didn't I see it happen myself during a county semi-final, when a man had his head split literally in two and our beautiful bottleman applied the healing balm.
The Prof replies back: Yes. Um, I think you might be confusing 'made-up stuff' with 'reality', Ted—
Ted interrupts: Ah, ya blackguard, you know nothing! I never trusted a man in glasses anyway. They all think they're intellectuals or something, knowing more than the common man. Well, they don't! Pol Pot had the right idea...
The Prof gets impatient: This correspondence is now closed. For ever.

Why is it that … players always claim they had 'a point to prove today' after winning a match? Do they ever just go out and make their best effort to win the game? Or what?
Clara O'Meara, Tara

The Prof says: This is what professionals know as 'spouting clichés', a rare linguistic disability wherein the sufferer automatically quotes one of a variety of well-worn hackneyed phrases. Other favourites include 'we've been training since last summer', 'at the end of the day the real winner was hurling' and 'I foresaw my own death in a vision last night'.

Why is it that … the prisoner on the camp 1960s' TV show of the same name never just captured No 1 and forced him to explain how to escape from the island? Surely this would have been more effective than running around, getting trapped in red phoneboxes and squashed by that big blob thing that used chase his boat.
Lucky Shiels, Sunset Strip, LA

The Prof says: I think you may be missing the fundamental *raison d'être* of the programme, Lucky, in that it was less a straightforward show than an existential meditation on whether we have any influence on the events that shape us. Patrick McGoohan's character, No 6, was a sort of Everyman, thrown into a bizarre, Kafkaesque situation whereby nothing made sense and thus reflected the innate meaninglessness of human existence … hang on a second, is this question about GAA or not?

● ●

The arts
and culture

MOVIE
the goalpost

Films and GAA; the cinema and the playing pitch; the stars of the silver screen and the giants of the game. Never really had too much in common, to be honest, except for the proliferation of violence, bloodshed and salty language which is a common feature of many edgy modern films and practically every match ever played.

Ken Loach's Cannes-winning *The Wind that Shook the Barley* opens on a hurling match, before the bastard Tans wind it up before the allotted time is played. Neil Jordan slipped a mention of hurling into *The Crying Game*, while *Clash of the Ash*, though not feature-length, was an enjoyable, truthful representation of the same sport in recession-era Cork. Back in the 1950s, John Gregson – who, according to my mother, was a suave, handsome devil – starred as the eponymous Rooney, a suave, handsome devil who played inter-county hurling. And *Taffin*, a memorably dreadful Pierce Brosnan thriller from the 1980s, featured a brief scene of a hurling match.

But we need more than that. We must strive for a day when the GAA is as prevalent a cinematic subject as sex, war, the Mafia, outer space or prim Regency ladies in frilly bonnets gossiping about eligible bachelors. We must look forward to that glorious moment when an Irish director, on scooping the Academy Award for Best Film, leaps onstage, hits Billy Crystal a clatter, grabs the mike and roars, 'A cháirde gael! Tá an áthas orm an Oscar seo a glacadh ar son an scannán *Camán Everybody: The Secret Hurling Life of Buddy Holly*. Three cheers for our gallant opponents, *Titanic II: Refloated*. Hip, hip, hooray!'

That moment may be a way off yet, but remember: it's a seventy-minute match, Ger, so patience is our watchword. In the meantime, I'll get the tuxedos dry cleaned.

REAdING the GAMe

GAA fans are quite an articulate and educated bunch in general. So given their love of reading and concurrent primordial lust for all things Gaelic, it's unfortunate that books on the subject have been pretty thin on the ground.

Actually, that's not the full truth – the *number* of tomes has never been a problem. You can't turn around without bumping into the latest collection of stats from the East Tyrone Institute for Collation of Obscure Match Results, handsomely bound in cheap white cardboard. Peek behind that and you'll spot a riveting history of the St Irrelevant Club in the Orkney Islands, founded by a blind leper missionary from Westmeath who subsisted on sloeberries and hurley hoops for two years.

No, it's the quality that presents a problem. GAA books are inevitably either statistical information presented with no context, maudlin reminiscences down Made-Up-In-Retrospect Lane, picture-books aimed at American tourists and native simpletons, bland 'Greats of the Sward' hagiographies (the writers are constitutionally obliged to use that term), self-lacerating autobiographies by recently retired stars, or a mixture of the above. A sort of overly sycophantic statistical run-through of self-lacerating past greats as they reminisce in a maudlin fashion photographs.

And...action!

Some more ideas for any budding *auteurs*

Jack the Ripper (18)

Terrifying Gothic fable about a demented trainer known as Jack the (Jersey) Ripper, who is determined to whip 'de biys' into shape by any means possible. Little do they realise this includes such horrors as running up and down the steepest hill in the county for four hours, and being sadistically eviscerated in their own bedrooms.

The Three Stooges in the Full-Forward Line (Gen)

Anarchic mayhem as Curly gets his head caught in the net, Larry misses an open goal and Moe knocks himself unconscious off the goalpost.

Charles Kickham's *Knocknagow*, I suppose, had some connection to the early days, while morose poet and sterling junior goalkeeper Patrick Kavanagh dropped a few references to Gaelic games throughout his oeuvre. More recently, Tom Mac Intyre's play *The Gallant John-Joe*, revolved around a former footballer. There have also been some decent biographies and even the odd stab at Nick Hornby-style contextualising of the games within a broader cultural framework.

But damn it, they still ain't getting my literary juices flowing. Despite the inherent artistry and dramatic scope of our games, the roll-call of great GAA literature remains virtually non-existent. I feel we need a broader palette to work from. Why, for instance, is there very little GAA poetry (excepting those collections of interminable, cliché-riddled 'ballads', which obviously can't be considered poetry in any proper sense)? Why has no one taken upon themselves the task of expressing the unknowable soul of our glorious games in verse form? Like this, say...

'Dark/the bright grey darkness of winter's gloaming, roaming/round the goalpost/post-effervescence of unwieldy ire/the man/the control the black black shirt and red/like death red bloodred like death redder than love and/redlikedeath the card/is raised you/ are sent off.'

Of course, if you want to be really pretentious, nothing beats a good haiku. The seventeen-syllable template can be difficult to conform to, but teaches discipline and helps concentrate the mind – excellent preparation for those crucial last few minutes when you're defending a two-point lead with thirteen men. And the wind is agin' you. So...

Training Day (18)

Gritty thriller about a corrupt veteran of many years' championship experience, who's given the job of 'training' the team's new hotshot corner-forward one 'day'. Sort of thing. The naïve newcomer is shocked when his mentor suggests some ruthless strategies, but with that crucial relegation dogfight on the horizon, he begins to be tempted...

Mulholland Drive (15)

Dreamy, disconcerting opus from David Lynch. Liam Mullholland is on his way to his first day in a top administrative post within the association. But the drive seems to stretch to eternity, as he is waylaid by a grotesque coterie of journalists, county board PROs and Strategic Review Committee members.

146

'Sullen though I was at our defeat, I lied to keep up a façade.'

Heart-rending stuff, pithily expressing that sublimely tragic moment of loss, when you're fed up and want to look for excuses, but your team-mates are acting all 'mature' and 'big in defeat', so you have to pretend not to be horribly childish and emotionally stunted. Apparently, this is socially unacceptable.

Poetry is not, of course, the only form through which an appreciation of the finer points of Gaelic games can be expressed. Our dramatists and novelists have long held their own in a crowded literary midfield, though personally I think a slump set in once that Rodney Boyle fella started winning awards. However, we must bear in mind that the majority of sports-book readers are men, and the majority of men don't like fiction or the theatre, preferring the lumpen pleasures of biographies and documentaries about shark attacks and crap like that.

We must, therefore, combine the literary and the factual to make any impact on the book-buying public. I propose a history of Clare hurling during Ger Loughnane's tenure, written in the experimental cut-up technique and terrifying, hallucinatory style of famed beat writer and chronic junkie, William Burroughs. Dystopian madness, violence, terror and hysteria? Yep, that about sums up the average day on the farm with the Banner boys back then.

The Longest Day (12)

Robert Mitchum's most famous, moving performance, in this slow-moving epic about one man's struggles to stay awake during a Dublin junior hurling Division 6 relegation decider.

Shallow Hal (12)

Sharp satire about Hal, a top inter-county footballer who seems to have it all: stardom, a bucketful of medals and a pretty good job that he would never have got on brains alone. But that's not enough for this grasping cur, and he's soon agitating for professionalism and whining to the press about 'sacrifices'. Viewers may find some scenes (of money-grabbing) disgusting to the point of nausea.

Now available in paperback or corner-back –
some mouth-watering GAA tomes

Crime and Punishment
Harrowing accounts of miscarriages of justice, taken from Croke Park politburo memoranda. Includes the infamous Colin Lynch Affair of 1998 and that time my U14 team thought one of our players had been sent off but he actually hadn't and we never got the chance of a replay.

The Time Machine
Bizarre fantasy from sci-fi pioneer H.G. Wells about a deranged Dublin football fan who yearns for a return of the all-conquering 1970s team. Or even the reasonably decent mid-1990s vintage. He invents a fantastical machine which can manipulate the space-time continuum, but can it go one better and drag Jimmy Keaveney out of retirement?

The Canterbury Tales
The earliest extant work of GAA literature, this famous saga follows the adventures of a ragged collection of pilgrims, including The Crofter, The Absentee Landlord and The Secret IRB Man, on their way to the first ever All-Ireland final. Wrytten Entyrhly in thise Anhoying Ye Olde stihle of Wrything.

Far from the Madding Crowd
Disturbing story of one young Junior B hotshot who, feeling the pressure from well-wishing locals, takes refuge in the cupboard under the stairs with a small transistor and four bottles of gin. He thus escapes the invasive crowds, but

I Was a Teenage Werewolf Half-Back (12)
B-movie horror classic ends in tragedy as promising young half-wolf starlet howls at the press box before eating the ball.

You Only Live Twice (Under the Backdoor System) (Gen)
Seamus Bond, crack centre-forward for Her Majesty's Secret Games Development Committee, must use his wits, and a bagful of hurling-related gadgets, to defeat his foe – Viktor Melyankova McEneaney – and help his side top the round-robin group. And there's an attractive young lady in a replica jersey and bobbly hat waiting for the full-time whistle…

encounters fresh problems – like where the hell to get some tonic and lemon in a cramped cupboard under the stairs…

Paradise Lost

Milton's endless (and fairly unreadable) epic poem about the trials and tribulations of lost souls seeking redemption and a state of grace. Yes, it's Fermanagh footballers, bound in the fiery maw of failure, suffering the infernal torments of poor shooting and low self-confidence, and yearning for salvation from the infinite hell that is the Ulster championship.

Gulliver's Travels

The rousing adventure of a fair-to-middling inter-county player called Gulliver who can't get a start for his own county, and ends up playing for their greatest rivals through a fortuitous (indeed suspicious) sequence of events, including a timely job offer and his engagement to the daughter of the county chairman.

Critique of Pure Reason

Brilliant philosophical dissertation on thought, language and the subconscious, packed full of big words with which you can impress your friends in heated coffee-house debates. It asks all the important questions, like 'What is the sound of one hurley clashing with itself?' and 'When Ger Canning says something utterly ridiculous but Michael Duignan isn't around to hear it, has he actually said it?'

À la Recherche du Temps Perdu (Remembrance of Things Past)

Colossal ten-volume work in which a reclusive Mayo man retires to his cork-lined room to pen an exhaustively detailed account of his life following the county team. And he still can't quite remember them winning Sam Maguire.

Bootsie (15)

Cross-dressing comedy starring Dustin Hoffman as an out-of-work midfielder who dresses in drag to get a place on his local camogie team. Trouble starts when he falls in love with the hard-hitting centre-back.

Meet the Parents (15)

Hilarious comedy about a guy whose plans to marry his sweetheart are thrown into disarray when her father learns that he never played GAA as a young fella. Robert De Niro stars as the rabidly anti-soccer man who thinks the Ban still applies – and that includes his daughter!

The play's the thing

Samuel Beckett is one of the most highly respected dramatists ever, his bleak, nonsensical doodlings fascinating critics and bewildering everybody else. But old Sam probably wouldn't have been the best man to bring GAA to the theatre. We want people to show passion and vim, not stare glumly into dying embers and proclaim the universe to be meaningless. Like, that really puts a dampener on post-All Ireland celebrations.

Contrary to popular presumption, though, Oscar Wilde would have been a great man to chronicle Gaelic games on the stage and, indeed, a great man to have in the dressing room. He was a big, hefty fella, not averse to throwing a few punches if ticked off, which is always a good start. He was also quite a zealous nationalist. His witty repartee would alleviate any pre-match tension and help strengthen that crucial team bond, while he'd never be short of a piquant quip to direct at an errant referee.

Oscar's razor-sharp mind and sparkling dramatic skills could combine to produce a penetrating portrayal of the GAA – with a few smart lines thrown in to amuse the plebs.

The Importance of Getting in the First Dig

by Oscar Wilde (aesthete, genius and All-Star corner-back, 1894)

SCENE: *A dressing room in West London, decorated in the sumptuous, baroque stylings of the age. Two louche young men loll about on chaises longues, smoking impossibly long French cigarettes and gazing absently into the distance. They are dressed in frilly, Spandau Ballet-type shirts, frock-coats and white togs with a stripe down the side. Their boots lie on the ground. Suddenly, one stands and begins to pace the floor, rapping the ground with his hurley.*

Lord Dorian McAfee, First Baron of Ballyswaggart: I say, pumpkin. We should really be out there warming up, don't you think?

[*The second man sighs in a very effete manner.*]

The Right Honourable Michilín 'Bowsey' Crinklington: Oh, sit down, for God's sake. The only thing worse than being talked about for missing training is not being talked about for missing training.

Dorian: Quite so, Bowsey, quite so; but Coach Huffingford-Maison will not be pleased. I fear four extra laps to be our punishment.

Michilín [*swishing his cigarette smoke through the air*]: Ah, but there is the nub and the rub, my dear Dorian. The coach is afflicted with the peculiar malady of the middle classes; to wit, the inability to recognise that the condition of perfection is idleness. I myself never put off until tomorrow what I can possibly leave until the day after.

Dorian: Hmm … all this sounds disconcertingly familiar. Almost like you were quoting someone famous … But anyway, the crux of the matter is this: we have a game to play, and The East Indian Tea Company Sarsfields are out there now, ready to play it. Do we want this wan badly enough, Bowsey? Do we want it!?

Michilín [*leaping up and grabbing his Micro helmet*]: Well, why didn't you put it like that before? There is only one thing I cannot resist, my dear Dorian, and that is temptation. Let's crush them like bugs!!

[*He runs out the door screaming wildly, followed by Dorian. Close curtain.*]

Scene: *Dorian and Michilín limp in, covered in cuts and bruises, with glum expressions. Dorian holds a radio from which is heard, 'That's right, Michael. Like, we were never at the races. Sarsfields had obviously watched the Lumière Cinématographe*

footage of the last day, and done what they had to do today.' The two friends slump onto their chaises longues.

DORIAN: You didn't stay for the post-match analysis, then, Bowsey?

MICHILÍN: No. Nothing bores me quite as much as my own business. I am only interested in the business of others.

DORIAN: Well, anyway, it would appear that all our hard work has come to naught.

MICHILÍN: Quite the opposite, pudding. We may be lying in the gutter of championship dreams, but we are looking at the stars ... of next year.

DORIAN: Yeah, right. Make sure to tell that to my bookie when he comes to break my thumbs, won't you?

[Close curtain. The end.]

I write the songs that make the whole county sing

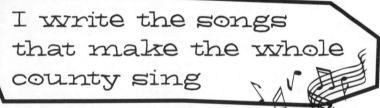

Despite the fact that Croke Park topped the *Billboard* magazine worldwide charts for the top-grossing gig of 2005 (that renowned GAA man, Bono, making a long-awaited return to his spiritual home – not), the county scene and decent music have never been too closely aligned. The half-time entertainment at matches, if present at all, tends to be a muffled tape-recording of some daft old tenor warbling away at 'The Rose of Tralee',

or a pipe band half-heartedly running through 'The Merry Ploughboy'. In recent years, admittedly, Croke Park has upped the ante somewhat in amusing the masses, but this generally involves some Macnas-style faffing about with giant *papier-mâché* hounds — something none of us really needs to experience — accompanied by music so loud, discordant and disorientating as to induce permanent nausea in the lowest eight tiers.

Among the fans, also, there is a dearth of musicality (farting three distinct notes and gargling the theme to *Dallas* to amuse your friends doesn't count as music). Unlike their soccer counterparts, GAA supporters don't sing moronic chants from the terraces, mainly because scores arrive frequently. You don't want to get caught out roaring 'Such-and-such is a homosexual' with gusto, only for someone to point out, 'Actually, he's just scored 2–2 in the past thirty seconds. *And* made the manager's wife pregnant.' Can you imagine the embarrassment? There have been one or two sporadic attempts at GAA chants, most notably 'Let's go, Limerick, let's go' during the Shannonsiders' semi-successful mid-1990s. Unfortunately, though, this was a bit of a damp squib, as people were never quite sure if it was a cry of allegiance or an exhortation for everyone to write bawdy, humorous verse in five lines.

Even the fact that Dermot O'Brien, one of Louth's 1957 All-Ireland winning side, was a bona fide showband star isn't much help, mainly because showbands sucked even worse than pipe bands half-heartedly running through 'The Merry Ploughboy'. However, music does dwell in one grand old institution: the county song. Normally reserved for when a team qualifies for the All-Ireland, these fall into one of two categories: either someone goes to the bother of writing an original song (e.g. the slightly presumptuous 'Five in a Row'), or rewrites an existing song with 'funny' lyrics. Hence we had, for instance, Mayo's alleged 'Babes' in 1996 with their take on Harry Belafonte's 'Banana Boat Song'.

I once wrote to a certain county board, proposing a radical shift in the way we look at county songs. I felt teams needed to diverge from 'those inane 'chanty'-type tunes, which follow the pattern of: bit of diddly-aye, childish chorus, sound of crowd roaring, more diddly-aye, 'funny' line, tacky

1980s-style guitar solo, etc.'. I offered to gather Shane McGowan and trip-hop guru Tricky in studio to write the ultimate in paranoid millennial-angst GAA anthems (with a Velvet Underground slant). For some reason, this certain county board never took me up on the offer. Must have been creative differences.

Regardless, GAA has become too cool for its musical expression to be left to the likes of Hairy Maurice and the Hungry Bastards, with their admittedly energetic hit, 'Let's Win this Wan for the Boys Below in Tomsie's'. For starters, the lyrics are all wrong. If it's not lists of players' names, it's lists of players' birthplaces, lists of locations for bonfires, shopping lists, *Schindler's List*, Franz Lizst, and so on. We need lyrics that capture the very essence of our national games in all their flawed glory. Or at the very least, some sort of rhyming scheme and a few references to bonfires. Musically, too, the county song must expand its horizons. Why not follow Paul Simon's footsteps and incorporate some Latino rhythms, with a nice bossa-nova version of 'El Bueno Rosa de Mooncoin'? Or maybe Duke Ellington could be disinterred to write a jazz symphony for Wicklow footballers. Schhmokin'! With so much cross-pollination of music today, anything is possible.

Failing that, you can never go too far wrong with a slushy, emotionally manipulative ballad. Ideally one featuring Elton John on piano, Mariah Carey and David Hasselhoff on vocals and, for extra street cred, that blondie little scobie Eminem on rapping duties. The title: 'We've Gotta Stop their Full-Forward (For the Children)'.

Cue wussy piano riff.

David: When the sky is dark ... and the game nearly lost ... You gotta hold on, baby ... no matter what the cost ...

Mariah: Whoooo-oooohhh ...

David: Just take my hand ... and I'll get you through ... 'Cause we can make it ... Baywatch Gaels abú ...

Chorus:

David: We gotta stop their full-forward ... for the children ...

Mariah: Ooooohhh ... for the children ...

David: We gotta clear good ball ... to the midfield ...

Mariah: Ooooohhh ... to the midfield ...

David: Baby, we got the right stuff ... if we want this wan badly enough

Mariah: Whoooo-oooohhh ...

David and Mariah (*gazing lovingly into each other's eyes*)**:** We gotta stop their full-forward ... for the children.

Cue Eminem listing every player's name and place of birth.

Long players:
some GAA/music link-ups

Shane McGowan: Great songwriter and even greater Tipp man, mentions hurling in 'The Broad Majestic Shannon'.

The Saw Doctors: Tuam football's biggest fans produce rabble-rousing music at its finest/most dreadful.

Donal Dineen: Ireland's hippest alternative DJ and stalwart junior footballer.

Kíla: Brilliant trad band with some hurling members.

Marilyn Manson: Well, he did get married in the home of the GAA.

Computer GAA-narrated

Since their conception three decades ago, computer games have provided intellectual stimulation, emotional sustenance and physical Repetitive Strain Injury to millions (of nerds).

And, in November 2005, this anti-social pastime was combined with GAA for the first time, as Sony released *Gaelic Games: Football* for something called the PS2 console. (I have absolutely no idea what that might be. Do you still have to put in a 20p coin to start games?) Endorsed by Croker and developed by the kindly and all-powerful Japanese megacorporation, the game enabled players to contest a single match or full season which, showing admirable thoroughness, even included the league. And, of course, you could manipulate the little pixelated characters to run, solo, kick a bad wide, draw a boot on someone, whatever. Sounds like smashing fun, all told.

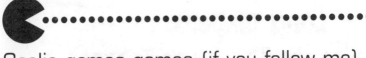

Gaelic games games (if you follow me) down the decades

Pong

The original and still the crappiest. I mean best. This simple game involves hitting a white rectangle (or 'sliotar') back and forth using two bigger rectangles (or 'hurleys'). Hugely enjoyable for about three minutes before the annoying 'bink!' sound and absolute lack of any purpose to proceedings makes players throw the console in the bin.

And the possibilities for further development are endless, really. For instance, I always thought about writing a programme to play a match on the internet, with friends across the globe, by using your office computer keyboard. Click the right mouse button to bring on a sub. Press F4 to hit your opponent a dig. Hit Save to, I dunno, make a save I suppose. Pull out the plug to abandon the game in controversial circumstances. A sound card could be crammed with generic platitudes like 'Ah, Jaysus, ref!', 'Pass it inside!' and 'We've been training for this one since the days of the IBM punch card tabulator, Marty.' Meanwhile, an Interview option would see the computer ask you banal questions after the game and simultaneously answer them from regurgitated *Sunday Game* quotes. Maybe some sort of virus could even be created to function as the ref: if you act the maggot, the game gobbles up your entire hard drive.

Then I realised that I hadn't a clue how to write code – or even what 'code' was – so the plan has been shelved indefinitely.

1942

Relive the thrills and spills of the GAA's glory years. You are Jack Lynch, future Taoiseach and lanky midfield maestro, and must collect six of the fabled 'Celtic crosses' in succession. But beware of your nemeses around Hell's Kitchen: the Foot 'n' Mouth Monster and Murderous Corner-Back.

Pacman

Brightly coloured fun as the boggle-eyed sphere chases those vital points around the screen (while letting the goals take care of themselves). Gobble some half-time energy drinks and then eat your opponents who've mysteriously turned blue. Or something.

What's the SCÓR?

The Scór isn't just the name of a record by quickly forgotten rap sensations The Fugees. Nor is it merely the title of a mediocre heist movie starring Ed Norton and Brando at his most lacklustre.

No, the Scór is the GAA's annual talent competition which brings a little culture to the masses. Granted, I haven't heard excerpts from *Eurydice* in a while, and the plays are more Brendan O'Carroll than Arthur Miller, but it provides us with some of life's finer pursuits: music, dance and innovative comedy involving a drunk who falls asleep and is mistaken for dead by the local idiot garda. And anyway, you want cultured? How's this for cultured?

Tank Trax

Gruelling test of strength, discipline and blind willingness to do the most utterly ridiculous thing ordered, as a late 1980s Mayo footballer engaged in bizarre training: pushing tanks around a car park. No actual football involved.

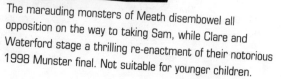

Mortal Kombat

The marauding monsters of Meath disembowel all opposition on the way to taking Sam, while Clare and Waterford stage a thrilling re-enactment of their notorious 1998 Munster final. Not suitable for younger children.

The Scór also features a poetry recitation, something I can't quite picture at monthly meetings of the average Chelsea supporters' club, unless mindless vitriol and xenophobic abuse have been recently reclassified as poetry.

Instigated to protect and foster our culture, the Scór includes traditional Irish music, dancing and that most revered of all native pursuits – the quiz. Irish people are indisputably obsessed with quizzes, in their many guises: book, pub, TV show or standing at a microphone in a freezing hall, trying to look cool in front of the girl who competed in the figure-dancing before the intermission. Which ain't easy in your school uniform and a haircut that would make Mötley Crüe blush.

Scór quizzes always featured at least one puzzler about The Beatles, at least 400 exhortations of 'no prompting, please', and at least three utterly ludicrous questions not even Steven Hawking could have answered. (I was once asked for the price of the newspaper without being told which paper. No shit.) But what really made the quiz was the quizmaster; or, more specifically, the quizmaster's hair, which was a glorious, and vaguely terrifying, wonder of the natural world. It was always just that bit too fuzzy to carry off the comb-over with real conviction, resulting in a weird 'plate-tilted-on-head'

Tomb Raider

You are a desperate inter-county manager who must try and 'raise the dead' by cajoling several former (and possibly deceased) players out of retirement before that big round-robin encounter. Hit Ctrl/Alt/Shift to enter their tombs, and Delete to erase all record of your crime from the police database.

Final Fantasy

You are ++SHANNONSIDER++, loyal Limerick fan, who must battle his way through decades of disappointments, near-misses and royal All-Ireland day screw-ups, in the vague hope that, some day, your dream will be realised and Limerick will actually win a final for once. Features digitally rendered Eamon Cregan for added realism.

effect. I have to say, the sight of a man with a sheer slab of greying fuzz sticking up off his head is one you don't easily forget. Just ask my therapist.

But the Scór wasn't solely about distressing tonsorial manifestations. The dancing was never less than enjoyable, with the threat of over-enthusiastic contestants stomping through the plywood stage giving an extra *frisson* of danger. The recitation was good, too; when that old favourite was wheeled out about the homesick immigrant dying before he could come home for Christmas, there wouldn't be a dry eye in the house. Though that may have had something to do with the critical levels of cigarette smoke. And as for the novelty act, who could forget the classic tale of the identical twins who keep getting mistaken for each other? Not me, anyway, as I must have seen variations of it about fifteen times.

Indeed, all this reminiscing has inspired me to make a stab at next year's preliminary rounds myself. I'm thinking of the full, unabridged version of *You Murdered Him, England, You Cold-Hearted Monster*, 192 sizzling verses crammed with the big themes of love, sex, death and betrayal … and some sultry maidens dancing seductively at the crossroads for good measure. Hey, you gotta give the people what they want.

Gran Turismo

High-speed thrills and spills as journalists break every acknowledged driving regulation in a breakneck attempt to catch two major matches which have been scheduled for the same day due to a fixtures cock-up.

Quake

Owing to shifts in the earth's polarity, an earthquake strikes on the day of the football league final, and Fraher's Field in Dungarvan, where the game is stupidly being played, begins to fall apart at the seams. Even more so than usual. Will the match be finished? Can the league trophy be rescued? Does anyone care among the approximate crowd of 157 humans and three stray dogs?

watch your language

Despite the fact that I didn't like it in school – purely a matter of personal taste, that's all – I've always believed in the importance of preserving the Irish language. Even back then, as I laboured through *Scothscéalta* like a bonobo ape struggling to master quantum mechanics, with only the fragrant beauty of my teacher preventing me from dodging the class altogether, I always *wanted* to be good at Irish. And I always wanted to like it, and wanted everyone else to like it too.

As someone cleverer than me once said, a people without a language is a people without a soul. Therefore, it's mighty important that we preserve the indigenous tongue, particularly in the face of an increasingly corporatised and homogenised world culture. And now, thanks be to Muhammad and his hydra-headed angels of death, the native language seems to be getting stronger and stronger. It enjoys a new-found cachet among suburban people with elaborate names like Fachtna, Maolíosa and Lasairfhíona; TG4 has carved out a quite alternative little niche for itself; and Raidió na Gaeltachta, in my opinion, carries the coolest music show in the country, bar none.

But for many years, the GAA was one of the few institutions in this country dedicated to the conservation of Irish, and – can you guess what's coming next, class? – were roundly ridiculed and abused for it. The insistence that, for instance, minutes and team lists be written *as Gaeilge* were lambasted as anti-quated, pointless and, in the all-encompassing 'modern ➡

world', discriminatory towards … well, I'm not sure, really. People who don't understand Irish, presumably. This reached its nadir for me when I read a column advocating the removal of the rule, as soon there would be kids of immigrants playing GAA, and how do you translate Apu Nahaseheemapetilon or whatever into Irish? (Answer: you don't, imbecile. Sort of like if you lived in Italy and played local soccer, they wouldn't have a fit worrying how to translate your name into Italian.)

But, as with so many things, the GAA stood firm in the face of these sneering ignoramuses. Sure, God love them. They don't know what they're on about, really, do they? Better to take an indulgent attitude towards this sort of nonsense, rather like the way one doesn't violently beat a dog for soiling the carpet, but merely smacks it on the nose and tells it to behave or there'll be no treats after dinner. Anyway, this hard-line policy has been vindicated now, with the acceptance of Irish as an official EU language and its increasing popularity, particularly among the young. So a hearty *bualadh bos* to members past and present for keeping part of our heritage alive. (Anyone who doesn't comprehend, go stand in the corner.)

Did you know that...?*

- …GAA founder Michael Cusack was also first treasurer of the Gaelic Union for the Preservation and Cultivation of the Irish Language?
- …the Gaelic League was founded in 1894 after the success of the GAA had influenced thinkers like Dr Douglas Hyde, a patron of the association?
- …RTÉ's commentaries on All-Ireland minor semi-finals and finals have been in Irish for many years at the GAA's insistence?

Actually, you probably did.

DON'T KNOW MUCH ABOUT PHILOSOPHY

It's time to get up close and pretentious with the world's first ever Tortured Philosophical Debate on the GAA.

THE MOTION:

That losing a match is of equal importance to standing on an ant.

Young man with stylised Trotskyesque goatee:

'This proposition, to me, is self-evident. There is no 'grand plan'; all is chaos; nothing has meaning. Therefore, losing a match is no greater nor lesser than standing on an ant.'

Goatee:
'No, it couldn't.'

Maudlin woman with lank hair and Venezuelan love beads:

'Yes, but when you say 'all is chaos' – could it not be argued that the chaos creates the order, and thus the meaning; and that the losing of a match inherently contains its own, self-made meaning?'

Obese man in ironic pop-culture T-shirt, eating a taco:

'I think both my learned friends are approaching this problem from the wrong perspective. It all depends on where both the match and the ant fit into the New World Order *Weltanschauung*. Who reffed this game? Where was the ant's body found? And did he know the Kennedys?'

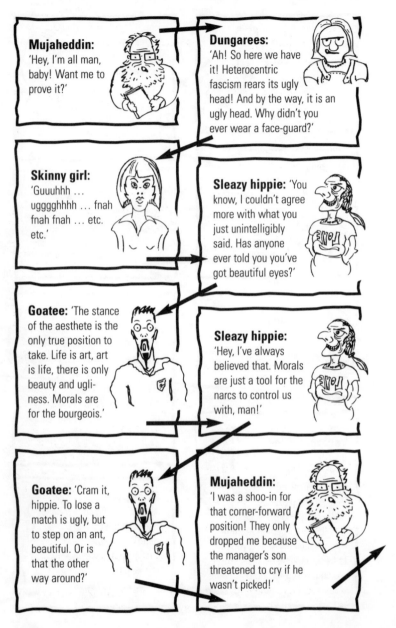

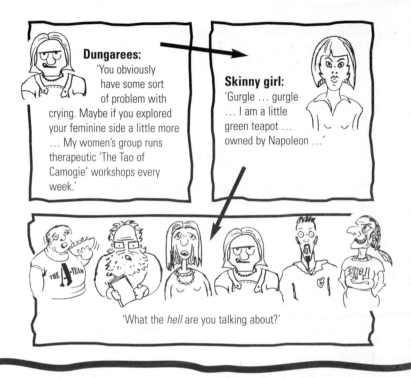

Dungarees: 'You obviously have some sort of problem with crying. Maybe if you explored your feminine side a little more … My women's group runs therapeutic 'The Tao of Camogie' workshops every week.'

Skinny girl: 'Gurgle … gurgle … I am a little green teapot … owned by Napoleon …'

'What the *hell* are you talking about?'

Jim Morrison's eerie statements from beyond the grave

'Before you slip into unconsciousness I'd like to have another kiss...'
…and also to recommend putting a fiver on Galway for the Liam MacCarthy. They're still available at 8/1 in some places and they're looking good, you soft, mad moon children.

'This is the end, beautiful friend; this is the end, my only friend, the end...'
…of Roscommon's interest in the championship, that is. Ah, they were unlucky though, lads. Could have had another three goals on a good day.

'You know that it would be untrue, you know that I would be a liar, if I was to say to you...'

...that the glory days are back for Cavan. Because tradition will only get you so far. At the end of the day, forwards win matches.

'The killer awoke before dawn; he put his boots on and he walked on down the hall...'

...pausing briefly to knock the door off the hinges on the way out. Jaysus, he was well psyched up out there today, wasn't he?

'There's a killer on the road, his brain is squirming like a toad; take a long holiday, let your children play...'

...and actually, the U14 selectors were only saying the other night how they can't find enough kids to fill a team. So get 'em out from in front of the telly and down to the field with a hurley in their hand, lads.

'The old get older and the young get stronger, may take a week or it may take longer...'

...and that can't really be good for the game, can it? Like, you'll never beat experience, but a lot of these lads, they're married, they've a young family, trying to start up a business, they just don't have time for the training, sure it's gone mental now...

'When the music's over ... when the music's over, yeah ... when the music's over...'

...it's time to throw in the ball and get the match underway! Yeeahhoooo!! Come on, lads! Get stuck into them early!

'Love me two-time baby, love me twice today; love me two-time girl, I'm gone away...'

...gone, but not forgotten. Thanks be to Jaysus for the new championship structures. Giving the so-called 'weaker' deceased rock singers another crack at it, and sure what's the point of putting in all the physical work in my graf-fitied Parisian grave if I only get one shot at it? Hah!? Tell me that, with all your schooling.

The look

DUBLIN

HAIR WE GO, HAIR WE G

DO IT FOR THE JERSEY

GAA jerseys have become something of a fashion item in recent years, adorning the bodies of the handsome and beautiful everywhere from college campuses to foreign cities to (God save us) the crowd at Wimbledon.

And speaking of campuses, what the hell is the idea behind that skull and crossbones logo on the UCC jerseys? Since when have teams been allowed use such weird and subversive designs? What are we educating here – a bunch of crazy long-haired hippie punk teenagers? Sure, the ban on shirt advertising went the way of the dodo years ago (except for that last surviving animal I munched on last Christmas – extinction tastes *so* good), and the beloved sash is now sadly restricted to beauty pageants and marchers in the Stonewall parade. And yes, the sleeves now have all manner of squares and crests and 'Ard Mhacha' or whatever in faux-Celtic writing. But dammit – and call me a traditionalist if you like – some things are sacred. The body of the jersey *must* be one of the following designs: hooped, plain or vertical stripes. Make all the adjustments you see fit, squeeze whatever trimmings you can onto the sleeve; just don't tamper with a classic.

The history of on-field GAA fashion

1560 BC: The 150th Tailteann Games are suspended for a fortnight when someone points out, 'You know, it might be easier to work out who's winning if the teams actually wear different colours. Just a suggestion.'
Two sets of hemp and rushes strips are quickly rustled up.

Dahling,
it's simply *wonderful*!

What is the funkiest jersey design out there? Should one opt for vertical stripes over hooped, simple black-and-white over eye-melting colours, clean lines over cluttered fiddly bits on the sleeves? I got one of my fashion VBFs to run the rule over each county's shirt – here's the verdict.

Antrim: The jerseys are saffron. Enough said.

Armagh: Fatally hampered by the fact that their colour is neither truly red nor orange, falling uncomfortably between the two.

Carlow: The world's most eye-boggling jersey, made with forty per cent real neon, is an incredible day-glo concoction bearing a remarkable resemblance to a water-ice.

Cavan: What is there to say about dull blue that anyone really wants to hear?

Clare: Much heated debate in Asian sweatshops when Clare unveiled their new design in 2000. And yes, the big 'V' thingie did make them look like they were wearing capes. Thankfully, the traditional centre stripe has since been brought back, with added epaulettes.

1690 AD: The Boyne League final ends in controversy when two members of Jacobite Óg are found in the colours of their opponents, Orange Invaders – those colours being orange. They are hanged, drawn and quartered, which really plays hell with the stitching on their outfits.

1829: Famed lawman and hard grafting midfielder Daniel O'Connell makes popular the 'tight breeches, flouncy shirt and unkempt, Romantic hair' look during his epic series of games against Landlords Abú. Eight million peasants race out and snap up trendy replica kits.

Cork: One of the classics, really, restored to former glory by ditching that big stupid 'C' on the sleeve. Duuh! C is for Cork!

Derry: Like the oak leaf itself, this is plain, dependable and just a tad boring.

Donegal: Deducted points for having almost exactly the same jerseys for the past decade (change is everything, baby).

Down: The all-time coolest GAA jersey, dark red and black combining for a poignant comment on love and mortality. Possibly.

Dublin: Mixing sky-blue and navy, apparently, is 'just not done', but that old Dublin cockiness lets them away with it. Though there is some debate among symbologists as to the true meaning of the 'three castles' motif.

Fermanagh: Boring old green; they never stood a chance. (See also entry for Leitrim.)

Galway: Only one redeeming feature: the cute little picture of a sailing ship on the sleeves. Aaw.

Kerry: It's a famous old shirt, right enough, and they tend to have a greater fondness for the long togs, which is obviously a good thing.

• •

1947: More controversy when a Cavan man gets a life suspension for playing without the regulation flat cap. He protests his innocence, claiming, 'Someone robbed it off me when we all threw our caps up in the air to celebrate a scrambled goal … in grainy black-and-white.'

2183: Mordor Centaurus, the reigning Galaxion IV hurling champions, launch their new kit design at a lavish function on the second moon of Saturn. The silicon-kryptonium alloy fabric is implanted with super-intelligent microchips that actually play the game for you, thus allowing players more time for intergalactic astral travel and battling giant spiders on the Sea of Tranquillity. And some woeful hard physical training as well.

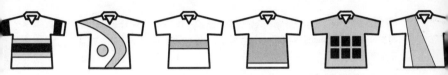

Kildare: Cool and clean, with simple lines and almost glacial perfection. If only Kildare's football could match their bright whites.

Kilkenny: With those vertical black 'n' amber stripes making the players look like extremely skinny two-legged wasps in helmets, Kilkenny's jerseys really stand out from the crowd. As you'd expect from extremely skinny two-legged wasps in helmets.

Laois: Tired old blue-and-white – Laois are done for from the get-go.

Leitrim: See entry for Fermanagh.

Limerick: Dull, dull green, not helped by the brief inclusion of the saddest shirt logo in history, the astronomically lame: 'Drug Free – Cúl!'

London: Damned by dwindling player levels and falling standards, London also suffer the misfortune of wearing Limerick-esque green.

Longford: Well, at least they don't wear Limerick-esque green. And that's as good as it's gonna get.

Louth: Reasonably smart red with white trim. The style used to be somewhat redolent of soccer shirts from the 1940s – like what the original owner of Billy's boots might have worn – but sadly isn't any more.

Mayo: Not bad, though severe visual disorientation may be induced by bright red and green being so close together.

Meath: Fairly humdrum green and gold, and they lose marks for the daftness of those macho short-short sleeves a few years back.

Monaghan: See entry for Leitrim, but change 'green' to 'white and blue'.

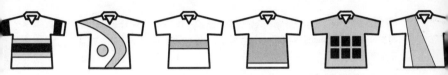

Offaly: Awarded bonus points for basing their kit on the colours of the national flag. Immediately lose bonus points for the poverty of the design.

Roscommon: At least they're bright, though the colour veers unnervingly close to that of Big Bird.

Sligo: Classic black and white, reminiscent of silent movies, the early work of Cartier-Bresson or a freshly washed pillowcase that's fallen into the mud. Don't you just hate when that happens?

Tipperary: Another grand old design, one relatively unaltered for decades. As they'd say themselves, you'll never beat tradition…

Tyrone: Rather like their neighbours Derry, this is solid, functional but a bit dreary. They won't thank me for saying that, will they?

Waterford: There's just something about a mainly white ensemble that makes me go weak at the knees. In a strictly heterosexual way, I hasten to add.

Westmeath: Maroon gloom. The most unflattering colour in the known universe, sadly.

Wexford: The hallucinogenic purple and gold combo has always brightened pitches and they've upped the ante recently, with a weird 'liquid metal' effect followed by the 'ran in the wash' look.

Wicklow: As with many of their forward-lines, it's 'nul points' for Wicklow's uninspired effort.

HAIR WE GO, HAIR WE GO, HAIR WE GO...

Up until relatively recently, there weren't really any distinctive haircuts to be seen on GAA fields. This is because up until relatively recently, everybody in the whole world had the exact same style at any one time. It was the law or something. But from the 1970s, things loosened up – man – with flaming sideburns, 'helmets' of hair and a veritable smorgasbord of disgusting mullets. The 1990s saw the crop orthodoxy prevail to some extent, but this decade has seen signs of renascent individuality.

World-renowned crimper and feared Junior D hatchetman, Pierre de Rocquefort-Higgins, lists his most memorable GAA hairstyles (giving it a little *zhoosh* while he's at it).

John Lynch (Tyrone)
Era: 1980s
Style: Enormous, Eurovision-style shaggy blond mane.
Fashionableness (yes, it really is a word): Considering the time, and the fact that Ulster is about ten years behind the rest of the country, surprisingly high.

Plunkett Donaghy (Tyrone)
Era: 1980s
Style: Not quite as enormous, Eurovision-style shaggy blond mane.
Fashionableness: See above.

Jimmy Barry Murphy (Cork)
Era: 1970s
Style: Extremely tight buzzcut.
Fashionableness: Low, given that every other male in the western world resembled one of the Hardy Boys during this decade. But he looked very cool.

Niall Patterson (Antrim)
Era: 1980s/1990s
Style: Leo Sayer bubble perm.
Fashionableness: I'll repeat that – Leo Sayer bubble perm.

John Duffy (Donegal)
Era: 1990s
Style: Dashing *Last of the Mohicans*-style half-pony (breech-load musket and buffalo skin chaps optional).
Fashionableness: Not very, but it still looked damned heroic.

Ger Oakley (Offaly)
Era: 1990s/2000s
Style: Studenty ponytail, replete with overgrown, *The Onedin Line*-style sideburns.
Fashionableness: This look will always be stylish among science undergrads, organic farmers and mentally delicate society drop-outs.

➡️

John Madden (Tipperary)
Era: 1980s/1990s
Style: Dapper, boyish Nigel Havers-esque 'do.
Fashionableness: High, if you're an urbane Wall Street futures trader with a summer house at Martha's Vineyard. Probably less so if you're not.

Anthony Finnerty (Mayo)
Era: 1980s/1990s
Style: Mildly bizarre frizzy hair shaped like a skateboard helmet.
Fashionableness: Even lower than the Leo Sayer bubble perm.

Roy Malone (Offaly)
Era: 1990s
Style: Messy, jagged Britpop cut.
Fashionableness: Painfully hip.

Ciaran McDonnell (Mayo)
Era: 1990s/2000s
Style: Short ponytail, later followed by cornrows.
Fashionableness: Fairly low, but you have to respect any white man who'll wear cornrows in public.

John Horgan (Cork)
Era: 1970s
Style: Frighteningly blond, floppy locks, rather like golfing legend Greg Norman. Or wrestling legend Hulk Hogan.
Fashionableness: For the time, high. For now, low. By the standards of the golfing world, astronomical.

Colm Parkinson (Laois)
Era: 2000s
Style: Messy, jagged Britpop cut (*ref.* Roy Malone).
Fashionableness: Hip, though not quite as painfully.

Dedicated
followers of
FASHION

When I was a lad, I remember going to matches at which my younger brother and I would wear our county caps backwards, *à la* those Kangol caps which later became popular among boyband members and golfers trying to appear cooler than they were. And it was amazing how much this simple act of sartorial individuality stood out. All we did was turn our cheap nylon headgear backwards, but even that marked us, I can modestly recount, as hipper than the pack. (Though my septum bolt and facial tattoo might also have played a part.)

Such was the way of things back then, when the marching band's dapper epaulettes represented about the only style on show and expressing oneself through fashion meant choosing whether to tuck your check shirt

I'LL GET THE BEARDS IN

Facial shrubbery has been conspicuous by its absence over the past ninety years or so, ever since all those Edwardian gentlemen simultaneously decided to shave off their robust handlebar moustaches to mark the end of the Great War. This is a pity, as many of the GAA's founding fathers – and one or two of the founding mothers – sported fine, manly beards. The 1970s saw a mini-revival, with Scouser 'taches springing up here and there, but since then, players' faces have remained resolutely clean-shaven.

With the following notable exceptions.

into your Dingos or just leave it hanging out. The county colours were limited to flags, rosettes and those crepe-paper hats that invariably gushed a torrent of ink down your forehead when it rained. But now, musha, 'tis all changed, with a staggering inventiveness of costume, and the increased attendance of slaves to fashion, making the average GAA match a pageant of colour and style.

It all started to transform some time in the late 1980s, when headbands and decent, non-staining caps became a common sight at games. Soon, GAA fans were showing their colours in an astonishing variety of ways: capes and Arab-style head-dresses, face-painting, hair-spraying, Viking helmets, jester hats, hair beads, car and house painting, bumper stickers and US president-type car flags, those daft baseball caps with the clapping hands on the bill … and a veritable United Nations of national flags and banners. Goatee beards on the gents, cute plaits on the ladies and sexy, futuristic sunglasses on both became more common. I like to think I also helped push the process along with some dashing and revolutionary touches, such as winding coloured thread into my flowing locks, and hanging a small teddy bear off my belt in the same way mercenary soldiers store their grenades for easy access.

Jimmy McGuinness (Donegal)
Era: 1990s/2000s
Style: Standard goatee (beautifully offset by cascading dark curls to give an overall Musketeer effect).

Eoin Liston (Kerry)
Era: 1970s/1980s
Style: Big, bristling bear of a beard, as befitted a big, bristling bear of a man.

Hughie Emerson (Laois)
Era: 1990s
Style: Sometime goatee wearer. Also sometime wearer of mass of knotted curls.

179

And that's before we get to replica jerseys, which have long outstripped shirts, T-shirts, polo shirts (and, in some parts of Monaghan, the dismembered ears of their foes on a line of string) as the upper-body 'garment *du jour*' for the big match. The renascent popularity of the Dublin football team, for instance, was proven when Arnott's announced that the county jersey had started to outsell Arsenal United and Real Barcelona and them other soccer crowds. Then, of course, some people started upping the ante, swapping their local jersey for some incredibly rare 1970s Romania shirt, or obscure Paraguayan volleyball top, which corresponded with the county colours.

Of course, it hasn't been all good news on the aesthetic front. The sight of huge-bellied men waddling towards the ground was somehow more palatable when they were dressed in a polo shirt, rather than squeezed into a county jersey at least four sizes too small. And without being discriminatory, middle-aged supporters of both sexes look faintly ridiculous in a replica shirt. I don't know why, they just do.

But the improved sartorial standards are generally welcome, and not just to leering perverts looking to scope out some hot babes in the crowd. Matches are brighter and gayer now, which can only be a good thing: for the association, for the future of the games, for the perceptual concept of colour itself, and for nervous match analysts who, fearful of offending someone with an actual comment on the game, can blather on about the boys and girls in their colours instead. ■

Liam Currams (Offaly)
Era: 1970s/1980s
Style: Trim, full beard, beloved of psychotherapists and geography lecturers everywhere.

Setanta Ó hAilpín (Cork)
Era: 2000s
Style: Extremely trendy, finely sculpted beard. A bit like Craig David has.

Ciaran Duff (Dublin)
Era: 1980s
Style: Straightforward, no-messing, meat-and-two-veg whiskers.

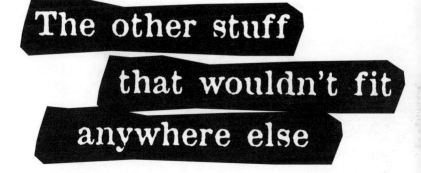

The other stuff that wouldn't fit anywhere else

Cult Heroes

We have, for a few decades now, been constantly hearing about the 'cult of the manager'. But what exactly does this mean in – as members of the political fraternity might say – real terms? Well, the dictionary definition of a cult includes 'a quasi-religious organisation using devious psychological techniques to gain and control adherents', 'ritual practices centred on sacred symbols' and 'intense interest in and devotion to a person, idea or activity'.

Now, if that doesn't summarise the average inter-county squad, I don't know what does. With the bossman as the sinister svengali, the players as blank-eyed devotees, and Sam or Liam as the godhead of their worship, it's clear that our top stars have been transformed into mindless automatons by power-crazed despots intent on domination. It's also clear that my life is in danger if I don't shut up right now.

But what if county boards appointed actual cult leaders to manage the team? Cutting out the middleman, so to speak. The following counties and charismatic basket-cases might just hit it off.

L. Ron Hubbard and Cork: Scientist, sci-fi writer, soldier, entrepreneur, messiah … the versatile Scientology founder could be the man to lead the Rebels to another double.

Sun Myung Moon and Tipperary: The cracked Korean never stops going on about how he's the rightful successor to Jesus himself, so should fit in well in a county infatuated with its own lineage and heritage.

David Koresh and any Ulster county: Used to feeling under siege at the Branch Davidian compound in Texas, Koresh could undoubtedly empathise with all those paranoid northerners.

Jim Jones and Waterford: After another season of 'so near and yet so far', even chugging back a bucket of poisoned Kool Aid might start to seem tempting.

Marshall Applewhite & Bonnie Nettles and Mayo: The founders of the Heaven's Gate cult were evidently able to persuade people that eternal bliss was but a short distance away, despite all the evidence suggesting otherwise. You see where I'm going with this.

Charles Manson and Clare: Technically not a cult leader, but Manson exerted a virtually messianic hold on his followers, who were willing to do anything for him. The right man to arrest the post-Loughnane slump?

Off your game

➔ Ah, the sending-off; where would we be without it? Avoiding grammatical conundrums such as 'Is it 'two sending-offs' or 'two sendings-off'?' for one thing.

➔ Now marked by the dramatic flourish of a red card, the sending-off has been part and parcel of our games for as long as men have felt the urge to clout other men. Which is to say, for ever. I wanted to bring you an in-depth, exhaustive history of dismissals, but such was their breathtaking volume that it would have necessitated the addition of 230 pages to this book, and the publishers were too mean to stump up. So you're gonna have to make do with some – though not all – of the sending-offs in All-Ireland finals.

➔ The first occurred, appropriately enough, during the first final itself on 1 April 1888. Could there be a connection between a date known for evil

jesters prancing about terrifyingly in bobbly hats with bells on the end, and what transpired that fateful day? One of the Galway team certainly felt like an 'April Fool' when he got his marching orders against Tipperary. Interestingly, the unknown solder was sent off for tripping the referee, a refreshing alternative to abusing the referee with non-parliamentarian language or locking him in the boot of the car.

➔ Hilariously – and rather sweetly – until 1895, a practice existed whereby dismissed players could return to the field with the agreement of the opposing captain. Isn't that nice? Then they abolished it, which wasn't so nice for an

anonymous Clare hurler sent off against Laois in 1914. Clare were obviously marking the beginning of World War I with a trademark abrasive performance. Incidentally, the sending-off was later appealed on scratchy black-and-white Kineopticon evidence.

➜ The 1916 decider featured a double dismissal, Tipp's Tommy Shanahan and Kilkenny's Dick Grace taking early showers. Well, there weren't any showers, but they got a good hosing down out the back of the stand. Cut to 1959, when Bobby Vinton ruled the charts, Marlon Brando had just become an icon of rebellion and Dick Carroll (Kilkenny) and John Barron (Waterford) were getting the line on the first Sunday in September. This begs some important questions. Why did so many people called Dick get sent off in finals? Why did so many people called Dick play for Kilkenny? And why have I not yet made one puerile pun on the name Dick in this entire piece? Questions, questions.

➜ In 1983, we enjoyed the king daddy bust-up of them all, when a record four players – Brian Mullins, Ray Hazley and Ciarán Duff of Dublin and Tomás Tierney of Galway – were sent off. This prompted much agonised soul-searching into What Has Gone Wrong With Football? for a good ten or twelve days afterwards. Speaking of Dublin, the most peculiar dismissal involved one of their number in 1995, when Charlie Redmond got an early bath. Cheeky Charlie remained on the field for a few minutes until the referee noticed his presence and sent him off again. Redmond reluctantly departed, albeit while shaking his fist and muttering dark threats about 'revenge from beyond the grave'.

➜ Then in 1996, Wexford's Eamon Scallan got the line in the victory over Limerick. Although a member of a team with the decidedly un-macho nickname of Yellowbellies, Scallan proved to be anything but when lamping some poor Limerick sod. The same year, the notorious Battle of the 21-Yard Line, which saw twenty-eight of the thirty participants involved in running scuffles for five minutes, resulted in dismissal for Meath's Colm Coyle and Mayo's Liam McHale. Cue some more agonised soul-searching into What Has Gone Wrong With Football?, this time for, wow, at least a fortnight.

➜ The last final sending-off was Armagh's Diarmaid Marsden in 2003, after some argy-bargy with his Tyrone opponent. Armagh folk claimed that the dismissal was unjust, but Diarmaid shouldn't be too downhearted by the whole experience. He now joins a long, illustrious list dating all the way back to 1887. I mean 1888. ∎

WEATHER THE STORM, LADS

We've all suffered from stormy weather doing lots of nasty things, like messing up our hair, blowing over cars and soaking the new deep-pile shag carpet that's just been laid in the hallway. But none have suffered more than our beloved GAA players, with games being postponed and messed up left, right and centre (though it was hard to tell exactly, as the centre had been blown out of its usual location by a hurricane one night).

1255 BC: The ancient Annals of Ireland record that this year's Tailteann Games Junior C semi-final is abandoned after floods drown half the competitors, and drive the other half indoors in mindless fear of further retribution from Elector, the Great God of Lightning and Storms and Such 'n' Such.

AD 1847: The Landlord/Peasant Shield is called off as an unseasonably damp spell blights the potatoes and kills approximately 92 per cent of the population, leaving the Peasant selectors without their first 15,000 choices for full-forward.

1900 (OR 1901 OR 1902 OR SOMETHING, I'M NOT SURE):

The first All-Ireland final of the century is delayed for longer than the usual three years that these things tended to be delayed for back then, when the players refuse to compete for fear of ruining their fetching tweed caps and woollen britches in the rain.

1939:

The legendary Thunder and Lightning final isn't called off, per se, but could have been as the weather is nothing short of atrocious. The doughty fellows of Cork and Kilkenny ignore the rain, cold and danger of being electrocuted whilst standing too near the metal stanchions supporting the old Hogan.

1985:

Galway beat Cork in a low-scoring mud-drenched death match to qualify for the All-Ireland hurling final. Many of the players are never seen again.

2001:

Several opening round football league matches are cancelled owing to snow on the pitch, water on the pitch, frost on the pitch and evil spirits who want to eat your soul on the pitch. (According to some guy in the pub who wanted me to buy him drink.)

Oh brother, where art thou lining out today?

Geneticists call it 'The Familial Closeness Matrix'; traditionalists call it 'The True Strength of the Association Hypothesis'; cynics call it 'The Less-Talented Younger Sibling Bandwagon Paradigm'. I simply call it: 'Brothers Playing Together'.

Sets of brothers have represented their counties for absolutely ages. Ooh, we're talking, like, majorly *fadó, fadó* here. Indeed, the very first All-Ireland winning team, Tipperary in 1887, featured no fewer than four Meaghers. By Christ, they bred hard and they bred fast back in them days, didn't they? Equally as impressive, four Delaney brothers appeared on the Laois team beaten in the 1936 All-Ireland football final. Actually, they lost, so that's less impressive, now that I think about it.

Wexford were represented by a troika of legendary Rackards, though Nicky, Bobby and Billy sounded more like the members of an Alabama blue-grass band. A fourth, Jimmy, played in the 1951 Leinster victory and helped out with the rhythm section from time to time. Meanwhile, three Bonnars helped Tipperary to All-Ireland success in 1989 and 1991, though confusion was caused by the fact that all had remarkably similar-sounding names: Conal, Colm and Cormac. Must have been a nightmare for any commentator with a speech impediment and enormous hangover.

The great Offaly team of the 1990s was particularly fraternal. Apart from the three Dooleys and two Pilkingtons, there were also three Whelehans, two Troys and two Hanniffys. Though possibly not all at the same time. Their fierce rivals Kilkenny have also been studded with famous sets of brothers, including many Hendersons and Fennellys beyond number. And the Cats created brother-related history in 2000 when Willie O'Connor followed in Eddie's footsteps by hoisting the Liam MacCarthy.

The three Spillanes are probably football's most renowned brothers, and certainly football's most spiky-haired brothers. Interestingly, in the ill-fated 1982 final, Pat, Mick and Tom faced three Lowrys, two Connors and two O'Connors, the last four chaps all being related on both the mother's and father's sides. Now *I'm* confused.

The 1952 football decider saw the decidedly strange scenario of brothers opposing one another: Liam and Dessie Maguire represented Cavan, and Brendan played for Meath. I wonder how that affected dinner-table conversation in the days leading up to the match? 'Pass us the salt, there.' 'Think I'm passing the salt to one of the opposition? At this table it's every man for himself!' 'Mam, Liam and Dessie are being stupid and won't pass me the salt.' 'You three behave or there'll be no All-Ireland for any of you!'

Comical puzzlement was the order of the day – or year – in 1980, when identical twins John and Pascal Ryan featured on the Galway panel. So similar did these scamps look that selectors found it hard to tell them apart. This no doubt led to many hilarious escapades, in which the twins swapped jerseys, came on as substitute when the other was tiring, or stood together in front of the referee after he had sent one off, staring in an unnerving way and intoning, 'You cannot send me off. I multiply when I am angered...' More recently, strikingly similar Armagh pair, John and Tony McEntee, could have pulled many of the same amusing stunts, though Cork's Ben and Jerry O'Connor circumvent any confusion by wearing different-coloured helmets. Jerry's is the black one, right...?

Across the sexual divide, sisters have also been doing it for themselves. Siblings Eileen Lawlor and Margaret Slattery of Kerry won a phenomenal nineteen All-Ireland women's football medals between them, while Kilkenny's famous twins, Angela and Ann Downey, must have racked up something like 263 medals during their *über*-successful camogie careers. An utterly staggering *eight* Kehoe sisters played camogie for Wexford (and one of them is the mother of soccer star Kevin Doyle).

And harking back to John and Pascal Ryan, their sister Ann played in the 1993 All-Ireland final. Unfortunately, she didn't possess her brothers' eerie twin-based powers, and Galway lost. ●

We had a job to do and we done it

There is a perceived notion among certain ill-informed types that GAA players are thick muckers who can barely write their own names – and it's about to be smashed. Check out this stellar inter-county line-up.

1 **Tom Mac Intyre (Cavan)** – writer

2 **Robbie Kelleher (Dublin)** – economist

3 **Francis Mulligan (Kildare)** – professor of physics

4 **John Browne (Cork)** – dentist

5 **Kevin Moran (Dublin)** – professional soccer player and businessman

6 **Jack Lynch (Cork)** – Taoiseach

7 **John Wilson (Cavan)** – Tánaiste

8 **Liam Hayes (Meath)** – newspaper editor and publisher

9 **Gerry McEntee (Meath)** – surgeon

10 **Jim Gavin (Dublin)** – army jet pilot

11 **Dermot Earley (Roscommon)** – UN army commandant

12 **Trevor Giles (Meath)** – physiotherapist

13 **Barney Eastwood (Tyrone)** – professional boxing manager

14 **Tony Hanahoe (Dublin)** – solicitor

15 **Joe Brolly (Derry)** – barrister

Speech boys

Controversy seems to dog certain politicos, particularly if they like making dramatic, attention-grabbing and, most crucially, utterly stupid speeches. But had the likes of Enoch Powell or Louis Farrakhan been GAA fans – fairly unlikely, when you think about it – they would have known how badly speeches can backfire. Winning captains saying the *cúpla focal* on receiving the cup is a uniquely Gaelic, and uniquely contentious, tradition. While most are well received, some strike such a wrong note that only sound-sensitive alarm systems and certain breeds of dog can comprehend them.

One of the most infamous GAA speeches of recent times was given by Anthony Daly after Clare had won the 1997 Munster hurling final. Revelling in victory and keen to stick it to Tipperary opponents who had lorded it over his county for decades, Daly announced, 'We're not going to be the whipping boys of Munster any more!' Needless to say, Tipp took great umbrage at what they perceived to be ungracious triumphalism, Daly protested his innocence, but the consequent bad blood remained for years. The following week, a different province saw the same story, when Wexford captain Rod Guiney parroted Daly's words after victory over Kilkenny. But this time it was sort of old hat, so everyone pretty much ignored the speech and instead had a laugh over the fact that the speaker's name was Rod.

Many speeches are used as a platform for airing grievances or having a go at someone, which happens on a regular basis in GAA circles. In 1993, the Kilkenny All-Ireland winning captain, Eddie O'Connor, started screeching about how his team deserved a holiday and how mean old Croke Park refused to pay for it. Everyone got embarrassed and stared at the ground until O'Connor finished his tirade. Four years previously, Cork football captain Denis Allen had pulled the same trick, with a vitriolic spiel against the 'boys in the crow's nest' who had never had faith in his side. No one was quite sure to whom exactly Allen was referring: journalists, GAA big-wigs, Russian spies gathering intelligence for Moscow from the roof of the Hogan? It could have been anyone. Again, everyone got embarrassed and stared at the ground.

*?!**&

There have been many non-contentious speeches down the years – Joe Connolly's memorable 1980 speech *as gaeilge*, for instance – but the safest way to avoid controversy is to keep it short and sweet. Which reminds me of a club-mate who, on reluctantly agreeing to add some post-acceptance words, simply remarked, 'Uh … three cheers for the opposition. Hip hip hooray. Thanks.' Couldn't have put it better myself.

YOU'RE NICKED!

GAA lore is full of cool nicknames, which may be representative of the famed Irish facility with language, or the fact that fellas surrounded by other fellas all the time tend to have trouble leaving behind an adolescent mentality. Either way, these are some of my favourites.

William 'SKINNER' Meagher (Laois) – the thin end of the wedge

Pat 'WEDGER' Meagher (Tipperary) – the wedge itself?

Terence 'SAMBO' McNaughton (Antrim) – political correctness a little late in reaching the Glens

Micky 'SPIKE' Fagan (Westmeath) – a prickly character

Dick 'DROOG' Walsh (Kilkenny) – bolshy great malchick who fillied real horrorshow

James 'SHINER' Brennan (Kilkenny) – shine on you crazy diamond

Michael 'GAH' and Paddy 'BALTY' Ahern (Cork) – proprietors of a Cusack Stand curry house?

Colm 'GOOCH' Cooper (Kerry) – the ultimate goal-poocher

Cormac 'THE VIKING' Bonnar (Tipperary) – plundered many defences

Tommy 'THE BOY WONDER' Murphy (Laois) – holy child prodigy, Batman!

Pat 'AEROPLANE' O'Shea (Kerry) – up, up and away

Diarmuid 'THE ROCK' O'Sullivan (Cork) – on which Cork's church is built

Martin 'GORTA' Comerford (Kilkenny) – he has the hunger

Ger 'SPARROW' O'Loughlin (Clare) – soared to success

Eoin 'BOMBER' Liston (Kerry) – on a mission to destroy

Michael 'BABS' Keating (Tipperary) – from boy to man

M.J. 'INKY' Flaherty (Galway) – read all about him

Tim **'ROUNDY'** Landers **(Kerry)** – dat's righ-yatt, Butty!

Paddy **'ICY'** Lanigan **(Kilkenny)** – one cool customer

Michael **'HOPPER'** McGrath **(Galway)** – team-mates with a Rabbitte

Tom **'GEGA'** O'Connor **(Kerry)** – the GAA's first gega-star

Michael **'DUXIE'** Walsh **(Kilkenny)** – look away, look away, look away Duxie-land

End game

The end has always been one of the more crucial components of matches. It's the part where we find out who won, for instance, note the final score and sometimes sneak off early to beat the traffic.

And dramatic, controversial or just plain chaotic endings have been more common than one would suppose. As far back as 1890, the Cork hurling captain was taking his lads off the field because their Wexford opponents had become 'too physical'. Admittedly, a Cork player had his toe broken by a wild pull, but the important thing to bear in mind is that he was in his bare feet at the time, which is just asking for trouble. But while the injury was Cork's, the insult fell to Wexford, as the Rebels were awarded the game.

Three years later, and there was more Cork—Wexford brouhaha, when an actual riot broke out after a Corkie fouled an opponent. Several players were injured, and once more Cork refused to continue. The big babies. It is unknown whether any Peelers were required to quell the disturbance, but presumably they would have done so in a comically speeded-up fashion, rushing around with a big fire-hose and bumping into each other like the Keystone Cops — as was, I believe, common police practice at the time.

Going against convention, Galway were actually beating Kerry in a replay of the 1938 football final, as opposed to losing a decider yet again. However, it all went a bit Pete Tong towards the end when the crowd — tum-tee-tum — invaded the pitch, thinking the final whistle had blown. Did nobody among them possess a watch? Anyway, the game was resumed after ten minutes of confusion.

This sort of craziness always seems like something from a bygone age, so it feels almost strange to mention Offaly's famous pitch sit-in of 1998. Who can ever forget that surreal moment when, with Clare hanging on for dear life and Offaly hunting them down like crazy Cajuns who've been at the moonshine, the referee accidentally finished the match four minutes early? I mean, I still think about it every now and again, and I didn't even see it — I was out the back playing with the dog at the time.

People power raged against the machine with a sit-in protest, and it all looked like great fun. I half-expected to see a few acoustic guitars whipped out, the bong passed around and 'Blowin' in the Wind' sung by some bearded hippie. But unlike the hippies, these people actually got some results: a replay the following Saturday.

Marching season

It's an integral part of the big match build-up, a mysterious, almost spiritual event unique to Gaelic games. But how much do you really know about the pre-match parade?

1. There is uncertainty about its origins, but one of the earliest was when Tipp and Galway hurlers marched in military formation before the All-Ireland final of 1887. Which was actually played in 1888, for no very good reason, as was the way of things back then.

2. Often there were several bands involved, as each county brought one and sometimes two. The Cork and Cavan teams that contested the 1945 All-Ireland final paraded after no fewer than five bands, which is just doing the dog on it altogether.

3. Kilkenny marched with sixteen men in 1959, the cheeky little monkeys. John Gregson was filming scenes for his part in *Rooney* (see section on Movies). Kilkenny lost the match, and later regretted not insisting the studio hire Alan Ladd instead. Or at least Sal Mineo.

4. Meath's Brian Stafford used the parade as an opportunity to change his boots before their 1988 replay against Cork. His team-mates didn't even notice, as they were too busy sizing up the Cork players' heads and working out the necessary force required to rip them off.

5. Limerick broke off early from the parade before the 1996 decider against Wexford, paying a double penalty: they looked like total eejits running around while the parade continued and Wexford won the cup. Limerick had displeased Ar Tane, the Great God of Parades and Marching and Stuff.

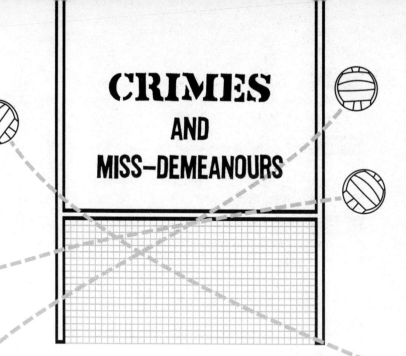

CRIMES
AND
MISS–DEMEANOURS

The penalty. The ultimate test of nerve, will and the ability to kick a ball between the posts and under the crossbar while evading the goalie. A place where boys become men, men are found out as boys, and boyish men find out how manly a boy they really are. Sort of thing.

There have been many exciting penalty-related moments in GAA history, but I'm feeling in a particularly sadistic mood, so have decided to concentrate solely on those that were missed. So take a deep breath, run up to the spot nervously and take your best shot … or worst. The penalty is death.

1940: The penalty kick is introduced in football and the semi-penalty (with three players standing on the line) in hurling. Our story begins.

1953: Bill McCorry famously misses a penalty for Armagh against Kerry in the All-Ireland final. Later immortalised as The Groan After The Saved Shot That Was Heard Around The World.

1974: Liam Sammon misses for Galway against Dublin, the first time he's ever done so. Unluckily for him, the miss now gets shown on sports nostalgia shows roughly once every three days.

1982: Mikey Sheehy misses for the Kingdom in the 1982 final against Offaly, who are inspired to victory. Sheehy isn't too perturbed, though, as Kerry just dust themselves down and go on winning titles for several more years. Speaking of which…

1986: Tyrone's Kevin McCabe balloons his shot over the bar, giving the northerners a seven, as opposed to nine, point lead. Big mistake, as Kerry win easily.

*** SPECIAL CHARLIE REDMOND SECTION ***

1988: Only manages a point against Meath in Leinster final.

1992: Over the bar again in All-Ireland final against Donegal.

1994: Shot is saved in All-Ireland defeat to Down.

*** END OF CHARLIE REDMOND SECTION ***

1991: Keith Barr skews his shot wide in the final game of Meath and Dublin's epic saga. Not helped by the fact that Mick Lyons gallops beside him in the run-up, waving his arms like a hyperactive goose that's been at the green Skittles.

1997: Probably the one and only penalty miss of D.J. Carey's career. Davy Fitzgerald pulls off a wonder save, then capers about like an ebola-crazed rhesus monkey.

2002: Oisín McConville misses at a crucial time in Armagh's final tilt against Kerry. But he makes amends by grabbing the historic match-winning goal. The ghost of Bill McCorry is finally put to bed.

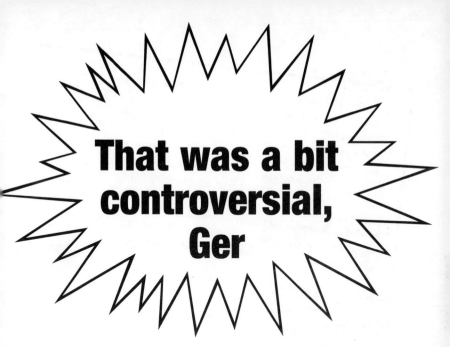

That was a bit controversial, Ger

Controversy. The midget musical genius and all-round bull-goose looney, The Artist Formerly Known As The Artist Formerly Known As Prince, sang all about it on one of his earlier albums (called, I believe, *Controversy*. Funny, that). Now, you're probably thinking, 'What the hell has midget musical genius and all-round bull-goose looney, The Artist Formerly blah blah blah, got to do with a GAA story? In all likelihood, His Purpleness knows very little about Gaelic games. Although to be fair, *Sign O' The Times* was a cracker. And you would be right – dead right. But it made a neat little intro, don'tcha think?

Anyway, we have seen more than our fair share of GAA controversies over time. To list them all here would be impossible; mainly because I am, fundamentally, a very lazy man. So here's a choice selection for you instead.

> Johnny Flaherty's hand-passed goal that ultimately won the 1981 Liam MacCarthy for Offaly was alleged to have been 'illegally transferred to the greater net-ular region by unlawful usage of the lower arm area and environs'; or 'thrown'. Offaly denied any misdeeds, but not too energetically – like, they'd won the cup, so what did they care?

The entire 1998 hurling championship was punctuated with controversies, including but not limited to: Ger Loughnane's bizarre and inflammatory radio comments, ructions and red cards at the Munster final, the Colin Lynch suspension, Marty Morrissey and Lynch's grandmother, the famed three priests, allegations of Munster Council machinations, Pat Hartigan at the racetrack, the notorious sixty-eight-minute match, and Babs Keating and the 'sheep in a heap'. Great craic, all told. (Interestingly, Babs' return to management for 2006 coincided with another eruption of controversy involving Loughnane, which again touched on administrative shenanigans, incendiary radio interviews, Marty Morrissey, the clergy and quite possibly some sheep arranged in a heap-like formation as well. Spooky.)

A few years back, a bunch of Roscommon footballers made the front pages of a particularly sleazy tabloid when, on a team-bonding trip, they got drunk together and played pool. *In the nude.* Now, I take as dim a view of media prurience as the next man, but *nude pool*? WTF!?

During one International Rules tour to Australia, Graham Geraghty applied an abusive racist epithet to his marker in a practice game. In fairness to the Meath man, he apologised immediately and explained how it had just happened in the heat of the moment. But the Irish management didn't exactly cover themselves in glory with their unperturbed response, which soon degenerated into the usual trick of blaming the media for the whole thing.

In 2003, Páidí Ó Sé talked himself into trouble, in a rare unguarded moment during an interview, when describing Kerry supporters as 'the roughest fucking animals' you could meet. Kerry people took umbrage, as did various rough animals – grizzly bears, hyenas and mountain yaks among them – who resented being likened to slavering hordes in green and gold livery. Páidí went on to compare himself, somewhat conceitedly, to Nelson Mandela on RTÉ News. Maybe it's best to stay away from the whole interview thing for a while, Páidí.

Brian Whelehan was famously marked absent from the 1994 All-Stars team, despite winning that season's Hurler of the Year award. Red faces all round for the selection panel … or there would have been, if anyone had known who they were.

Spin that record one more time

In 2002, Rory Gallagher – then of Fermanagh, now of Cavan – equalled the football championship scoring record which had stood for a full forty-two years. His colossal 3–9 total against Monaghan was a momentous achievement for several reasons: football has become more defensive in recent years; he was playing for Fermanagh at the time; and if, as sources indicate, this is the same Rory Gallagher who earned fame as a blues guitarist, he's actually been dead for about fifteen years.

➔

But Rockin' Rory is merely the latest in a long line of shooting stars who blasted their way into immortality and gave operators of those unwieldy manual scoreboards one almighty headache. The previous football record-holder was one John Joyce, who cracked home 5–3 for Dublin against Longford in 1960. The highest confirmed score in the hurling championship, a whopping 7–7 against Antrim in 1954, was set by Wexford legend Nicky Rackard, while the fragrantly named Andy 'Doric' Buckley scored 7–4 for Cork in the 1903 final. Others have neared that total down the years, but unfortunately, newspaper accounts weren't the most reliable, so reported totals vary wildly. And to think of the torture inflicted by some of my editors if I so much as left out the *fada* on someone's name.

Across entire championships, Eddie Keher's name shines brightly. The Kilkenny legend accumulated, for example, an astonishing 6–45 (57) in five games in 1972. Offaly forward Matt Connor struck fear into the hearts of goalkeepers everywhere in 1980, when he scored 5–31 (46) in four matches, an average of 11.5 per game, which is pretty goddamn incredible considering the size of a football goals and, more pertinently, the size of the average football goalkeeper.

Most of the above-mentioned featured a goodly proportion of frees, so it is to Tyrone we must venture for what is surely the record score from play in football, Frank McGuigan's fantastic 0–11 in 1984. Showing all the style, wit and aesthetic sensibility for which Ulster footballers are rightly renowned, McGuigan's total incorporated points off the left, right and from the hand. Another phantasmagorical feat of scoreboard-bothering derring-do was achieved by some chap called Jimmy Kelly in 1905, when scoring seven goals in just thirty minutes. And did you know that some other chap called Martin Kennedy is rumoured to have scored ten goals in a 1920s league match for Tipperary? Unless you're using the same network of snitches and stool pigeons as me, I doubt it.

The 2006 season also saw some notable scoring sensations,

such as Henry Shefflin's 1–13 for Kilkenny in the All-Ireland hurling semi-final against Clare, Alan Kerins' 4–2 for Galway in a qualifier against Laois and Eoin Kelly's 0–13 for Tipperary against Limerick, including a Munster championship record of 0–9 from play. Mattie Forde, meanwhile, notched a scarcely feasible 0–9 from play (out of a total of 0–12) against Meath in the Leinster football first round which, if it isn't a record of some sort, really should be.

Of course, statistics are naught but the devil's numerical vomit, and many extraordinary scoring records* have been set without actually scoring much at all. For instance, Ger Cunningham scored a point direct from a puck-out whilst on an All-Stars tour of Amerikay. Though even that pales into insignificance when set beside the strange and wondrous case of Pat 'Cocker' Daly who, according to legend, kicked a football so hard in Croker that it actually went *over the Railway wall*. Holy crap. What were they feeding them in those days?

(*By 'records' I mean 'not really records in the accepted sense of the word'.)

NAMed ANd FAMed

The GAA has a place for every Tom, Dick and Harry ... even if they're not actually called Tom, Dick or Harry. Here are some players whose names won't easily be forgotten.

1   Stuart McKenzie-Smyth (Kildare)

2   Paddy 'Rusty' Rustchitzko (Laois)

NAMed And FAMed

contd

3   Ian Twiss (Kerry)

4   Lazerian Molloy (Offaly)

5   Shane Brick (Kerry)

6   Tony Scroope (Tipperary)

7   Moses Coffey (Wicklow)

8   Bill Sex (Kildare)

9   Morgan Nix (Kerry)

10   Setanta Ó hAilpín (Cork)

11   Joe Caesar (Tipperary)

12   Hubert Rigney (Offaly)

13   Eddie Rockett (Waterford)

14   Marius Stones (Offaly)

15   Hank Traynor (Meath)

CROWDED HOUSE

A recurring (and extremely tedious) aspect of big matches is the old conundrum of securing tickets. Nanoseconds after one's team qualifies for the decider, a reporter invariably grins to camera and says, 'The hunt for tickets is on now!' After throwing a half-full can of Special Brew at the screen in annoyance, the normal course of action is to begin the frantic search before some other punk gets his hands on your property.

But you might not be aware that, in days of yore, tickets were easier to come by than a beating from the landlord for not licking the mud off his boots. This is because attendances were tiny in the GAA's early years. For instance, a paltry 1,500 attended the 1889 All-Ireland final, a damning indictment of the fair-weather follower. Although most people were busy emigrating or starving to death at the time, so we probably shouldn't be too harsh. Crowds increased exponentially soon afterwards, though, with an impressive 11,000 at the 1909 hurling final and a scarcely feasible 32,000 at the 1913 Croke Memorial Fund final. I wonder how many people would turn up at a memorial match for me? Surely if some nobody like Dr Croke can swing that many, a great hero of the association like myself would be looking at hiring out the Maracana Stadium, no?

Record attendances for All-Ireland finals were set in the 1950s and 1960s, a time when the authorities weren't too bothered about crushing everyone into the ground like Japanese sardines. A phantasmagorical 90,556 watched Down play Offaly in the 1961 football decider, still the greatest Gaelic games attendance ever. My own dear old dad often remarked of this game, 'If you turned sideways for a moment, the crush was such that you'd be unable to turn back,' but the McManus children never really believed him, as he was prone to melodrama and exaggeration from time to time.

The myriad of pointless/completely insane competitions held throughout the GAA's history means, of course, a myriad of attendance records. For instance, the 1963 Grounds Tournament set the record for any rubbish competition ever: 42,337. The Oireachtas (which apparently still exists but never seems to feature any actual games) regularly drew attendances of 30,000 during its heyday about a million years ago. And the 1920s' revival of the Tailteann Games was reported to have crowds of 20,000. Though this was probably just made up by the organisers.

Moving further 'afield' (geddit? Another cracker from the Darragh J. gag-factory), the record GAA attendance on foreign soil is reportedly the 60,000 who watched Kerry footballers in Yankee Stadium in 1931. Surprisingly, the famed Polo Grounds All-Ireland of 1947 drew a meagre 34,941, but a fantastic 42,500 Cockernees toddled along to the 1963 Wembley Tournament finals, which seems unlikely ever to be matched because that competition has been disbanded for the past four decades.

Looking ahead, it should be interesting to see if the 2084 Centenary Final matches the attendance (59,814) of its twentieth-century predecessor. Someone let me know what happens if I'm already dead by that stage, would you? You'll find me buried under the Maracana.

Odds and sods

It's the age-old problem. You've inherited/found/come-across-by-other-means-I-don't-need-to-know a large sum of money and, being a greedy little tyke, are just dying to stake it on next season's GAA action.

But trying to predict who'll win the championship is like sitting ➡

Odds and sods

into a bath full of baby alligators: no matter how carefully you've covered all the bases, sooner or later you're gonna get a big bite on the ass. The usual means of divining the future – studying the form, extrapolating from past results, smoking opium and waiting for the answer to be revealed in a bizarre and garish dream – have proven unreliable at best, completely rubbish at worst. Therefore, I have used all my contacts and journalistic wiles to gather together a crack team of experts to collate, debate and extrapolate – and talk a lot of gibberish while they're at it. However, in keeping with my determinedly avant-garde aesthetic, I've spurned the usual know-it-alls, instead seeking enlightenment from the true Brahmins of the modern age – famous people.

Man United icon and piss-poor actor, **Eric Cantona**, has seen his fair share of battles (especially with opposing fans), so who better to pass judgement on forthcoming clashes? Le King declared, "Urling is not a sport – it is sirty men making love to a sliosar. 'Ow can you shoose between ze unstoppable and ze immovable? It is impossible, but we try, as we love it so.' He then stared moodily out the window and smoked some Gitanes.

Legendary glam rocker **David Bowie** has long been a fan of our games, as seen in his dedication of 'Sorrow' to Limerick hurlers. Talking to me from the early 1980s (when he was still fairly good), Bowie 'Ziggy'-zagged around the thorny issue of picking a winner, saying, 'Dunno, really – I kind of lost interest when Martin Quigley retired. But I do think Eoin Kelly can be a 'Starman' up front for Tipp – he's a real 'Jean Genius' when he gets the ball in his hand.'

Cerebrally challenged movie star and all-round degenerate **Charlie Sheen** was delighted to get my call, exclaiming, 'I'm delighted

Odds and sods ....

to get your call. No, really, I am – nobody calls me anymore, not even Emilio. Yeah, like *his* career was going somewhere until *Bobby*. Anyway, this is a tough one to call. I think it'll boil down to whoever has the hunger on the day, although a big wind might have a bearing.'

Big-haired TV crime-buster **Michael Knight** was able to chat through the amazing satellite link-up in his futuristic car KITT. Knight, who plays lanky crooner David Hasselbahnhoff in real life, yelled, 'Yo, Darragh James! Whatcha got for me?' When I pointed out that I, in fact, wanted something from him, he bellowed, 'I am *on it*, good buddy. Over and out!' and turbo-boosted off down the highway.

Seeking more intellectual analysis, I turned to intense, vaguely scary Russian chess grandmaster **Gary Kasparov**, who said, 'We need to change the structures – maybe allowing the so-called weaker teams to go forward by two spaces instead of one. And the likes of Tyrone and Kilkenny should be limited to one move only, perhaps diagonally.'

Slightly confused by Kasparov's ramblings, I asked deceased Nobel-winning dramatist **Samuel Beckett** for his thoughts. This man of few words had, er, few words to say. 'No. Yes. To be, to bee, too bee, two bees. Sting, beesting, be sting, be still. Still. End.'

So there you have it. The die has been cast, and the fat horses are preparing to leave the paddock … and sing. All that remains is for you to mortgage the house, lie to your partner about how you're spending the family money, and pick a side. Best of luck!

PS: If you meet Donny Panucci, you never saw me, capeesh?

TIME, GENTLEMEN, PLEASE!

It's unstoppable, unavoidable and liable to go on for ever, barring some sort of cataclysmic cosmic shift resulting in self-implosion. It's time, and people want to know it. So don't be 'week'; be 'hour' guest and spend some of your 'daily' bread on one of these beauties.

MEATH FOOTBALL HEART-ATTACK POP-UP CALENDAR: Flip the page and veer dangerously close to coronary arrest as a horde of marauding Meath men leap up at you. From the 1988 vintage in January to 1996's brawlers in December, there's a guaranteed rush of heart-stopping fear every month. **€19.99**

GER AND MARTY QUOTE-A-RAMA DESKTOP CALENDAR: Peel off a page each day to reveal another illustrative, amusing or downright crazy quote from Ger and Marty. Highlights include the classic 'There'll be no cows left alive in Leitrim tonight.' **€11.49**

JERRY O'CONNOR PERPETUAL MOTION FLICK-THRU HOME ANIMATION CALENDAR: Not especially good for telling what day it is, but does enable the owner to pretend they're watching footage of the Cork speedster in action by flicking through the pages at high speed and tricking the eye-brain connection. Might need to buy a supplementary calendar for date/month purposes. **€15.00**

SALVADOR DALI RIP-OFF ICONS OF THE SWARD CALENDAR: Penniless art-school graduate does reasonably believable pastiches of the famous surrealist's style on well-known figures. Joe Deane, Steven McDonnell and Tony Griffin are among those reinvented in imaginative and somewhat disturbing ways. **€21.99**

LOOLY'S HARDWARE STORE FREE-TO-VALUED-CUSTOMERS CALENDAR: The annual time-keeper from Festertown's premier sell-everything shop, showcasing a fuzzy picture of the local pitch, and printed on cheap paper previously used as cardboard casing for their vast supply of incredibly ugly Chinese ornaments. Free to anyone purchasing over €10 worth of home-decorating equipment.

TRIP DOWN MEMORY LANE NOSTALGIA-FEST CALENDAR:
Handsomely mounted product shamelessly cashing in on the public's inherent sentimentality, featuring several poorly repro-duced photographs of famous players down the ages with absolutely no context or explanation. Includes genuine faux-handwritten font. **€24.99**.

The boardgame

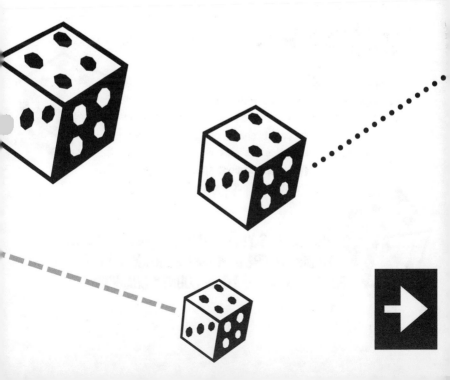

THE €64 MILLION BOARDGAME!!*

We all have a dream. For some, it's to capture the jackpot in the Lotto; for others, to tunnel out of their jail cell with a plastic fork. But the ultimate dream for most people is simple – to win the county championship. That dream is usually not realised for various reasons, including medical ailments, dodgy refereeing decisions and confinement to a jail cell without easy access to plastic cutlery of any description.

BUT NOW IS YOUR CHANCE TO BID FOR GLORY, TO DREAM THE IMPOSSIBLE DREAM, TO REACH FOR THE STARS – TO BE COUNTY CHAMPION!!

NO OF PLAYERS: Up to four (two subs).

PLAYING EQUIPMENT: Board, dice, red and yellow disciplinary cards (actual board, dice and cards must be purchased separately).

HOW TO PLAY: Toss a coin to see who goes first. After that, each turn is decided by whoever gets a sly dig in first. Throw dice to move around the board and follow the instructions there-after. If you land on a square saying 'Yellow card', you must stand for three minutes with a contrite expression on your face as one of the other players warns you about your future conduct. If you land on a square saying 'Red card', you must walk out of the room, shaking your head in disgust and kicking over a bucket of water by the door. Whoever reaches the Final Whistle first is crowned County Champion!!

START

1 You're put in the easy side of the draw. Move forward 3 spaces.

3 The county team are still involved in the championship. For some never-fully-explained reason, all clubs matches have been postponed. Miss a go.

4 Limber up nicely for the real thing with a few drubbings of carefully selected challenge opponents. Move forward 5 spaces.

7 Oof! A crashing tackle by the opposition hatchet-man in the first game KOs your star player. Move back 2 spaces.

10 Doctors confirm that the skull was only partly fractured. Move forward 2 spaces.

12 *Yellow card!* For persistent tugging of your marker's shorts.

15 A late own-goal ensures your first win of the campaign. Move forward 3 spaces.

18 A late own-goal ensures your first defeat of the campaign. Move back 3 spaces.

21 The club's sole inter-county panellist is bumped up to the first 21. All matches postponed indefinitely. Miss a go 15 times in succession.

23 *Yellow card!* For muttering lurid abuse about the referee under your breath.

26 Rumours of financial impropriety – spread by you – destabilise your opponents long enough for you to sneak the points. Move forward 4 spaces, then back 2 to make sure your karma doesn't get you later on.

29 All-in brawl during crunch qualifier is declared a draw. No move.

31 Sponsor provides shiny new jerseys in mid-season. Their stylishness, coolness and all-round wearability provide crucial gee-up to morale. Move forward 3 spaces.

35 Goalkeeping howler undoes all the good work of those new jerseys. Move back 3 spaces.

37   The county team is finally turfed out of the championship. No move, but heave a hearty sigh of relief.

39   *Red card!* For wrestling your direct opponent to the ground and dragging him through the mud by his nostrils.

42   Last chance saloon in the loser's group: you survive, barely. Move forward 2 spaces.

44   Star player's skull sewn together and he returns to the fray. Very gingerly move forward 3 spaces.

47   Dubious refereeing decision sees you through taut semi-final. The gods are smiling upon you. Move forward 4 spaces.

49   Internecine dispute about placement in the official team picture threatens to derail the bandwagon. Move back 3 spaces.

52   *Yellow card!* For muttering lurid abuse about your own team captain under your breath.

55   Big-day nerves play havoc with the first-half performance, not to mention the toilet bowls in the dressing room. Move back 2 spaces.

58   Big-day nerves placated by mass half-time dosage of soluble valium. Emerge a changed outfit for second period. Move forward 3 spaces.

60   Peep-peep-peep! It's the Final Whistle and you are **COUNTY CHAMPION!** Now get thee to the local hostelry – a lemonade, blood and poitín cocktail awaits in the bowels of the big cup.
PAR–TAY!! WOOH, WOOH, WOOH!!

FAREWELL ADDRESS FROM THE AUTHOR

I HOPE YOU HAVE ENJOYED THIS BOOK, AND HOPE EVEN MORE THAT YOU WILL ENCOURAGE ALL YOUR FRIENDS AND FAMILY TO PURCHASE A COPY OF THEIR OWN, INSTEAD OF JUST BORROWING YOURS.

IT'S NOW TIME FOR US TO SAY **FAREWELL** BUT NOT GOODBYE. THAT'S BECAUSE I'LL BE MAKING MY TRIUMPHANT RETURN TO THE BOOKSHELVES AND BESTSELLER LISTS, AND AS AN ANNOYINGLY UBIQUITOUS PRESENCE HOVERING ON THE PERIPHERY OF YOUR LIFE, REAL SOON. **MY FABULOUS NEW BOOK**, AS YET UNTITLED (AND, INDEED, UNWRITTEN), IS SURE TO BE ANOTHER ROLLICKING RIOT OF READING. SO SAVE UP THEM PENNIES, FOLKS. WHENEVER I GET AROUND TO THROWING SOME OLD RUBBISH TOGETHER, A GREAT EVENING'S ENTERTAINMENT IS GUARANTEED. AND THAT'S A GUARANTEE!*

IN THE MEANTIME, SIT UP STRAIGHT, FLY RIGHT AND WHATEVER YOU DO, FOR GOD'S SAKE KEEP IT COUNTRY. **CIAO, RAGAZZI**.

(*NOT A GUARANTEE IN ANY ACCEPTED LEGAL SENSE)

ACKNOWLEDGEMENTS

THANKS TO:

MY FANTABULOUS FAMILY FOR ENCOURAGING THIS
SORT OF NONSENSE FROM AN EARLY AGE. MY WIFE,
MAJELLA, FOR HER STERLING WORK AS CONSIGLIERE
(AND THE GREAT TITLE), AND ALL THE MACNAMARA
FAMILY. BUNRATTY PRINTWORKS! THE MANY
FRIENDS AND COLLEAGUES I'VE KNOWN AND WORKED
WITH, ESPECIALLY EOGHAN CORRY. CLAIRE ROURKE
AND ALL AT HODDER HEADLINE IRELAND. MY AGENT
JONATHAN WILLIAMS. DONAL MCANALLEN FOR HIS
FORENSIC PROOFREADING. MY ENGLISH TEACHERS,
ESPECIALLY SISTER DECLAN. EMLY GAA CLUB. NICKY
FOR THAT GOAL IN '87. ALL THE PEOPLE WHO LINED
PITCHES, CUT THE GRASS, SOLD LOTTO TICKETS AND
TRAINED US UNGRATEFUL BRATS.

AND FINALLY, THE THOUSANDS OF WOMEN WHOSE
SUPPORT ENABLED THE DEDICATION OF THOUSANDS
OF MEN.

MÍLE BUÍOCHAS!

The index

B

C

F

G

H

M

S

W

waddling men, huge bellies of 180
Ward, Tony, autobiography of xv
Waters and the Wild, The 4
weaker counties, so-called but there's nothing 'so-called' about it 82
weather
        inclement 101
        terrifying 186
Wilde, Oscar, surprising propensity for throwing punches 150
women, crippling fear of, found in golfers 74
women in GAA 44
women's football
        huge increase in popularity of 64
        name of, author's problem with 65
        quality of 65
wrestling as sublimation of homosexual leanings 8
writing, reasons for xv

X

Xena, Warrior Princess, junior version of 45

Y

Ye Olde Anhoying stihle of Wrything 148
your stomach, sick feeling in pit of 79

Z

Zola, Émile 7